Antonio Moniz, Kumi Okuwada

Technology Assessment in Japan and Europe

Technology Assessment in Japan and Europe

by

Antonio Moniz
Kumi Okuwada

KIT Scientific Publishing

Impressum

KIT Scientific Publishing

Karlsruher Institut für Technologie (KIT)
KIT Scientific Publishing
Straße am Forum 2
D-76131 Karlsruhe

www.ksp.kit.edu

Print on Demand 2016

ISBN 978-3-7315-0429-0
DOI 10.5445/KSP/1000048740

Contents

Figures

Tables

Foreword

António Moniz and Kumi Okuwada

This book consists of the proceedings and related discussions of a workshop entitled "Technology Assessment: A Stable Solution or Only Relevant Under Pressure?," which was held in Tokyo July 11, 2014. This workshop was jointly organized by KIT_ITAS (the Institute for Technology Assessment and Systems Analysis, of the Karlsruhe Institute of Science, in Germany) and JST_RISTEX (the Research Institute of Science and Technology for Society, of the Japan Science and Technology Agency) and also had the assistance of the University Nova Lisbon (Portugal).

In the announcement of this international workshop,[1] it was mentioned that the goal of technology assessment (TA) – which comprises one concept of interdisciplinary problem-oriented research, policy consulting (such as parliamentary TA), and public dialogue – is to lend support to society and policy making by promoting understanding of the problems related to the grand sociotechnical challenges of our time, as well as to assess the available options for managing them. Controversially, it could be useful to identify socially sound, "stable," resilient, and practical ways to deal with these technological challenges.

We can verify that many countries have shown interest in TA and TA-like activities since the 1970s (Vig and Paschen, 2000). This applies to the United States and the establishment of the Office for Technology Assessment at the Congress, as well as subsequently to other agencies in Europe,

---

1 http://eventos.fct.unl.pt/technologyassessmentandsimulation/home

such as TAB (Germany), POST (UK), and OPECST (France). As Hennen and Ladikas emphasize, "TA had originally been conceptualised as a procedure of scientific policy consulting, i.e. essentially a process of communication between experts and decision-makers. TA aimed to broaden the knowledge base of policy decisions by comprehensively analysing the socio-economic preconditions as well as the possible social, economic and environmental impacts of the implementation of new technologies" (Hennen and Ladikas, 2009:41–42). However, from time to time, these activities feared for their continuation, implementation, and consideration in both science and technology research and political processes (e.g., the Office of Technology Assessment in the US, the DBT in Denmark, and the IST in Belgium).

Currently, there seems to be an increasing demand in the European Union (EU) and in Japan for the ability to assess technologies. In 2011, the European Commission launched the PACITA project to support European countries in implementing and formalizing TA activities.[2] The Japanese Ministry of Education, Culture, Sports, Science and Technology (MEXT) established the SciREX program (Science for Redesigning Science, Technology and Innovation Policy) to start rethinking Japan's attitude toward science and technology and their impact on society,[3] and RISTEX initiated a program on the Science of Science, Technology and Innovation Policy.[4]

Many social issues have been discussed, such as the following examples: (a) the aging society, (b) global environmental change, and (c) the resilience of social systems. The Fukushima case created a push for more TA studies and the need for formal TA activity. For example, the National Diet of Japan Fukushima Nuclear Accident Independent

2 http://www.pacitaproject.eu/
3 http://www.jst.go.jp/crds/scirex/en/about/index.html
4 http://www.ristex.jp/EN/examin/stipolicy/index.html

Investigation Commission (NAIIC) formalized TA activity with a direct connection with the national Parliament, but there is still no TA unit at the National Diet.[5] As Koboyashi referes in this book at the last chapter, "to build collaboration with other TA-like activities in Japan, it is necessary to overcome major challenges. The most important one is that those in academic circles understand the characteristics of assistance provided for legislation and its difference from assistance given to administrative bodies" (p. 177).

In spite these attempts at institutionalization TA should be an analytical approach that should address both the direct effects and the indirect influence of technology development in our society. Such effects and influence would appear both in their positive and their negative aspects in society. It should cover a wide range of factors exerting influence on aspects of economics, environment, ethics, law, and culture.

The object of TA should essentially be the relationship between technology and society. This shared understanding constitutes the basis of the collaboration between ITAS, which conducts research comprising multi-faceted TA approaches on topics ranging from ethical factors to political ones, UNL, which promotes a PhD program on TA, and RISTEX, which promotes the social embedding of science and technology.

Assessment to Identify an Unforeseen Big Crisis

The emergence and quick diffusion of new scientific approaches and new technologies have brought about an increased diversity of objectives in TA. Because of the complexity of the contemporary social system, social risk has also assumed diversified forms. In this book,

5 See the article by Koboyashi in this book.

Taniguchi emphasizes the necessity of conducting assessment to identify an unforeseen crisis whose social impact would be extremely severe independent of its probability, such as the great east Japanese mega natural disasters and the Fukushima nuclear crisis. In this case, only a few stakeholders had recognized the risk.

There was a large gap between their understanding of risk and that of most people. After this crisis occurred, most people expressed their surprise, using words such as "unprecedented" or "unpredictable," despite having known of the previous such events in the world. Taniguchi describes that, in order to bridge this gap, some risk governance framework is necessary to relate their understanding and political decision making (p. 23 and followings).

Matsuo et al. describes that a process of joint fact-finding by the stakeholders should have been required before any political decisions were made after the big crisis (p. 89 and followings). On the other hand, thinking of risk concerning natural resources, including the economic aspect, Yarime introduced their trial visualization of material flow as a possible TA tool (p. 129 and followings).

After the crisis of March 11 (also known as 3.11) disclosures of risks have been more required in Japan. We have to look at availability and usability of them as preparedness measures. As Büscher mentions, it is increasingly apparent that the energy system transformation "poses socio-technical problems which require more than merely technical solutions. These socio-technical problems require, moreover, social solutions; both on the level of the energy system as a functional unit (of organizations, regimes and networks), as well as on the level of individual action" (p. 104). In this sense that would not be just a problem that only Japan would have to face. Many other societies with similar change processes have to deal with new risk management policies.

A Stable Solution?

As the pace of societal change has accelerated, it has become more difficult for us to find a stable solution to societal issues. Our sense of ethics also varies with social change, as do the necessity and acceptability of a specific technology in society. Thinking in terms of contemporary TA, it seems necessary that innovation agencies prepare some tools for recognizing such chronological changes in society and in its relations with technology. The same applies to other actors and institutions. Policy advisors, academics, and legislators also need such tools. We may also have to prepare other tools for making real-time or on-time assessment. Globalization requires us to think of diffusion to another areas and the impact on them and to undertake international comparisons. In this book, Yoshizawa describes his expectations for a new generation of TA, based on his review of world TA activities (p. 37 and followings).

Especially, TA of highly advanced forms of technology requires assumptions about the future society when they would be employed. This is the reason that foresight methodologies have begun showing some meaning in TA activities. Prior to the year 2000, attention was paid to technology roadmaps. Nowadays, however, foresight activities have become more important in thinking about the future of a society because in many cases the intended social situations would lead to the selection of new technologies (Yokoo and Okuwada, 2013). Germany and Japan are advanced countries that have developed many types of foresight tools. In current foresight activities, a back-casting type of thinking has been induced, reinforcing the existing forecasting type of methods. In this book, Kanou discussed a possible political simulation in a case of medical regulations. Simulation could be a useful tool in new type of TA that includes assumptions about future society.

The Experience with TA in Japan and Europe

In this workshop, the participants from Japan have emphasized the fact that the scope of TA discussion in Japan has historically been limited or trivialized. They have pointed out problems related to the fact that the widespread image of TA in Japan has differed from that found elsewhere. In Japan, the concept of TA is still very strongly associated with politics. This could have led to the fact that few Japanese researchers acknowledge to be pursuing the TA approach in their scientific activities.

However, at this workshop Kobayashi reported on recent TA activity for the Diet in Japan, and this experience is reflected in his chapter in this book. In his chapter, he describes his experiences until starting his TA activity at the National Diet Library (p. 163 and followings).

The articles from Scherz and Merz and from Boavida and Moniz present a different perspective. The first article is about established parliamentary TA institutions in Europe, based on the experiences and lessons described in the PACITA project (cf. Scherz and Merz, p. 57 and followings). The second reflects on some cases in countries where parliamentary TA has not yet been implemented but where TA activities have nevertheless taken place (see also Hennen and Nierling, 2014). Some similarities can be seen to the Japanese case (cf. 75 and followings).

Recent Trends from the Japanese Project “Science of Science, Technology and Innovation Policy”

Outside the discussions held at this workshop, the “Science of Science, Technology and Innovation Policy” program pays attention for other trends in related TA research.

Especially in some advanced countries that are in an unsound situation as far as national finances are concerned, an economic assessment has become regarded as being of increased importance in their recent innovation policy. The total economic benefit to society now more strongly influences the receptivity for technology, which may often differ from the provider's point of view. TA would afresh be regarded as important to presume validity of R&D investment for new technologies.

On the other hand, open data policy and big data have initiated a new era of assessment tools. Visualization and the capacity to reuse data have become more important features in assessments. For example, a large amount of disaster risk data has been accumulated in the aftermath of the 3.11 crisis in Japan and has been shown to the public as the geographic risk map. On the other hand, it should be mandatory that the results of R&D trials conducted with public funds are openly accessible as part of ensuring the accountability of public investments in advanced counties. TA tools should also transform such trials in the near future.

Based on the recognition of these trends, the program “Science of Science, Technology and Innovation Policy” in Japan has been managed toward realizing an evidence-based policy-making process. This program overlaps with the efforts to move toward a new era of TA.

One can observe that the concern for TA and TA-like activities has developed in waves depending on country-specific political circumstances, current frictions within the sociotechnical system, or catastrophes or accidents such as in Chernobyl or Fukushima. The argument is that TA-like activities represent a social response to technological challenges. Whether institutionalized or not, the capacity to handle technological challenges does imply the attitude to make decision makers aware of alternatives and to maintain the scientific capacity to reflect on several options. It therefore appears relevant to understand the conditions that must be met to establish TA permanently.

The organizers of the workshop invited researchers from Japan and Europe to reflect together on country-specific developments to identify the conditions that must be present to anchor TA in science, politics, and society:

- What are the triggers and barriers to establishing TA?
- Can technological accidents or disasters be more than the peak of a (TA) development?
- Would simulation play a role in foresight for TA?
- And what can countries with an established (parliamentary) TA learn from those countries that are currently institutionalising TA?

The aim of the workshop is to learn about different cultural conditions that have promoted the formation of a reflexive science. How important are sustainability, social acceptability, public participation, and environmental compatibility in interdisciplinary fields of research such as energy, mobility, or health? Is there an understanding of issues relevant to TA?

European-Japanese Institutional Collaboration Around TA

In Europe, the Institute for Technology Assessment and Systems Analysis (ITAS) of the Karlsruhe Institute of Technology (KIT) is known as a center of excellence on technology assessment (Paschen, 2000: 101). Its members have investigated TA methods and surrounding topics for a long time and suggested new types of methodologies for TA from a neutral perspective. They have helped spread TA activities all over the world.

According to the ITAS organizational objectives and mission, a specific type of research has been developed that is characterized as follows[6]:

- **Relevance for problems and practice:** With its research, ITAS ties in with the need for consultation on the impact of science and technology. Knowledge is developed against the background of societal problems, discourse, and upcoming decisions on technology.
- **Relation to the future and reflexivity:** As a basic principle, there is always a prospective aspect in the Institute's research since it deals with the future impact of human action and societal decisions.
- **Normativity and sustainability:** ITAS approaches the problem of technology assessment with scientific means. Ethical criteria and the general principle of sustainable development provide a stable guideline.
- **Inter- and transdisciplinarity:** The range of tasks of ITAS requires an interdisciplinary crossing of disciplinary borders and the transdisciplinary participation of stakeholders and citizens.

6 http://www.itas.kit.edu/english/research.php

In Portugal, and in accordance with the strategy of developing interdisciplinary competitive research, the School of Sciences and Technology (FCT) of the University Nova Lisbon focuses on the training of future engineers and scientists, promoting teaching and research that may be competitive at all levels. Emphasis is given to the need for students to become aware of the significant role science and technology play in the creation and organization of European society. The interest and commitment given to this area of intellectual inquiry by the School of Science and Technology closely follows those of reputed schools of engineering, such as MIT, Georgia Tech, the Karlsruhe Institute of Technology, and the University of Twente, all of which include the critical area known as STS (science, technology, and society), offered to students during several stages of their learning cycles (Moniz, 2012).

Consequently, the School of Sciences and Technology of the University Nova Lisbon has been a pioneer in terms of its educational vision, whether with respect to its undergraduate and master's level programs (several courses in the area of the sociology of technology and industrial sociology) or at the doctoral level (technology assessment). The doctoral program in technology assessment reflects a continuation of this two-decades-long commitment by the School of Science and Technology (Moniz and Grunwald, 2009).

The Research Institute of Science and Technology for Society (RIST-EX) has pursued the societal embedding of science and technology supported the relevant research projects. It started a research program called "Science of Science, Technology and Innovation Policy" in 2011, aiming to realize a more strongly evidence-based policy process. Since studies for policy design had been undeveloped in Japan, the incubation of its culture and expansion of research communities are also objectives of this program. Therefore, TA is an essential research issue in the "Science of Science, Technology and Innovation Policy" program.

These institutions agreed to cooperate in holding this first international workshop at RISTEX in Tokyo in 2014.[7] The subsequent step was publication of this book by KIT Scientific Publishing. The webpage announcing the event will be maintained by the University Nova Lisbon (UNL) for further joint activities. This has prepared the ground for new steps concerning TA. Meanwhile, in the frame of the European PACITA project on parliamentary technology assessment experiences throughout Europe, it was held the final conference in Berlin on February 2015. In that conference António Moniz, Go Yoshizawa and Michiel Van Oudheusden organized a session on "Technology Assessment in East Asia: Experiences and New Approaches" with the participation of some authors of this book. There they were underlying that "by placing the development in historical, sociological, and comparative perspective, the panel seeks to open a space for critical reflection on the potential, problems, and limitations of initiating TA in Asia and draw connections to science, technology and innovation governance processes in other knowledge based economies across the globe".

New steps can be developed in the near future by these institutions in such a way that collaborative activities and scientific research on TA could be conducted both in Japan and in Europe. The advanced training and exchange of experts can help expand TA capacity at a global level. Thus, we present to the reader this book containing the papers presented to this scientific dialogue to promote the mutual understanding of complex societies that are facing important new demands in terms of technological opportunities and societal changes. Such knowledge is beneficial to the scientific communities dealing with technology assessment and policy advice in innovative contexts.

7 http://www.ristex.jp/stipolicy/en/topics/20140711.html

References

Hasegawa, K. (2004), Constructing Civil Society in Japan: Voices of Environmental Movements, Melbourne, Trans-Pacific Press, 312 pp.

Hennen, L.; Ladikas, M., (2009), Embedding society in European science and technology policy advice, in Ladikas, M., ed., Embedding society in science & technology policy: European and Chinese perspectives (Ed), Brussels, Directorate-General for Research, 144 pp.

Hennen, L.; Nierling, L., (2014), A next wave of Technology Assessment? Barriers and opportunities for establishing TA in seven European countries. Science and Public Policy 41(2014)3, DOI: 10.1093/scipol/scu020

Moniz, A., 2012: Designing a Technology Assessment Post-graduation Programme: Experiences, Limits and Needs. In: Dusseldorp, M.; Beecroft, R. (eds.): Technikfolgen abschätzen lehren. Bildungspotenziale transdisziplinärer Methoden. Wiesbaden, pp. 357–370

Moniz, A.; Grunwald, A., 2009: Recent Experiences and Emerging Cooperation Schemes on TA and Education: An Insight into Cases in Portugal and Germany. In: Technikfolgenabschätzung – Theorie und Praxis 18/3 (2009), pp. 17–24

Moniz, A.; Yoshizawa, G. and Van Oudheusden, M. 2015: Technology Assessment in East Asia: Experiences and New Approaches, in PACITA, The Next Horizon of Technology Assessment - 2nd European TA Conference Book of Abstracts, Berlin, pp. 36-37.

Paschen, H. 2000: The Technology Assessment Bureau of the German Parliament, in Vig, N. and Paschen, H., eds., Parliaments and

Technology: The Development of Technology Assessment in Europe, New York, SUNY Press, pp. 93 – 124

Vig, N. and Paschen, H., eds. 2000: Parliaments and Technology: The Development of Technology Assessment in Europe, New York, SUNY Press, 399 pp.

Yokoo, Y. and Okuwada, K., 2013: Identifying expected areas of future innovation by combining foresight outputs, foresight, Vol.15 Iss:1, pp.6–18, DOI:10.1108/14636681311310105

Preface

Armin Grunwald

Technology Assessment (TA) has been invented and firstly practiced in the United Stated of America almost 50 years ago. Its very idea of establishing research-based policy advice on the use and consequences of the technological advance spread quickly among several countries in Europe but also to Japan. According to the different boundary conditions in the various countries with respect to technology governance, institutionalization of science and technology policy, political traditions and the status of citizen participation different TA approaches and concepts were developed, and different institutions were created. The diversity of constellations led to a diversity of manifestations of TA.

While this is a logical consequence of the very idea of TA it seems also necessary to develop a TA perspective beyond this diversity. Exchange and mutual learning on the various approaches and their achievements and limitations are essential for the international TA community to develop new ideas on concepts, methods and items, and to grow by attracting researchers from different disciplines and from regions all over the world.

There have been contacts between TA researchers and practitioners from Europe and Japan for decades. This exchange of ideas already has contributed considerably to the emergence of an international TA community we are witnessing now. The book "Technology Assessment in Japan and Europe" is a further step to strengthen exchange and mutual learning between these two and quite important parts of the world. I highly welcome this book as a major contribution to the TA communities of Japan and Europe but I also expect important signals beyond: on the way towards an international TA community.

Preface

Akira Morita

Innovation policy is being considered ever more important in the world. As evidence for this policy making process has become more important, the research program "Science for Science, Technology and Innovation Policy" was started in Japan in 2011.

In the summer of 2014, we held a workshop in Tokyo on technology assessment and related topics as a collaborative event between researchers from ITAS and members of our project. Technology assessment is regarded as comprehensive analysis of both the positive and the negative aspects associated with science or technology, including their secondary impact.

Technology assistance research should be employed for wider topics in the economy, environment, ethics, institutions, civilization, and culture. The data, methods, and models created as the result of this research should be such that they can be embedded in real political processes. In this sense, technology assessment is one of the important features of Science for Science, Technology and Innovation Policy project. I regret that very few sociologists have been working on technology assessment in Japan.

It is impossible to pursue technology assessment without a precise grasp of the social situation. The social system both in the EU and in Japan will undergo significant changes in the near future because of the inevitable transformations related to their population dynamics. The social implications of advanced technologies constitute a key facet to solving the social problems associated with such technology. Thinking of these future prospects, I feel that the chance for experts from ITAS at KIT and researchers from our Japanese program to hold collaborative discussions has been very meaningful. I hope that this book will help attract more people to participate in these discussions.

Preface

Shinichiro Izumi

In the summer of 2014, a workshop was held on issues related to modern technology assessment under the collaboration of ITAS from KIT (Germany), UNL (Portugal) and RISTEX. It is very meaningful that this book has been published as an output and record of the workshop.

At the1st World Conference on Science held in Budapest, Hungary, in June, 1999, and sponsored jointly by UNESCO and ICSU, the Declaration on Science and the Use of Scientific Knowledge (the Budapest Declaration) was issued with regard to what science and technology should be in the twenty-first century.

According to the Declaration, in the future science and technology should not only produce knowledge but broaden its attention with regard to how to use it. The previous function of science for knowledge is thus augmented by three new functions, namely by science for peace, science for development, and science in society and science for society.

The Japanese organization founded in 2001 and based on the spirit of science in society and science for society was the predecessor one of today's RISTEX. RISTEX is one of the divisions of the Japan Science and Technology Agency (JST). In contrast to the other divisions of JST, which primarily fund research and development based on knowledge from the natural sciences, RISTEX funds and manages research and development which directly address society. By operating and managing research and development program, RISTEX emphasizes that the results of this research and development are embedded in society.

Needless to say, assessment of the impact of each new technology on society is a basic part of our discussion of the relationship between science and technology and society. In 2005, the predecessor of RISTEX had an introductory book on technology assessment issued by ITAS translated into Japanese for our intensive study. I believe that the collaboration with ITAS at this time constitutes an extension of this history. I am aware that the social aspects to be coped with – with the assistance of technology assessment – have been emerging and expanding rapidly as a result of the rapid development of ICT and medical technology. I therefore strongly hope that another opportunity for collaboration between ITAS and RISTEX will present itself in the near future.

Part I

Examples of TA and TA-like Activities: Country-Specific Views

Technology Assessment and Risk Governance: Challenges Ahead in Japan

Taketoshi Taniguchi

Introduction

Today's socioeconomic activities are becoming more interdependent in an increasingly interconnected complex world with rapid technological progress. Different forms of modern technology pose risks of a systemic nature, which typically spread over more than one country and more than one sector, and may have effects across nature, technology, and the social system. While these risks may be relatively low in frequency, they may have broad ramifications for human health, safety, and security, the environment, economic welfare, and the fabric of societies. Secondary and tertiary social or economic consequences, so-called "ripple effects," are considered to be unintended or unforeseeable consequences in the eyes of the people or organization that causes the incident, on the other hand, to be unexpected consequences in the eyes of a victim. And it is easy for the interested party to be aware of the risks and benefits of science and technology, but not clear to almost all people in a complex society. These gaps in perception can create issues of societal risk of great complexity and ambiguity that may be hard to deal with. The Great East Japan mega-natural disasters and the Fukushima nuclear crisis have put this risk landscape of Japanese society into relief.

This paper outlines the political situation surrounding nuclear power in Japan after the Fukushima nuclear disaster, and discusses the role of technology assessment in nuclear risk governance and some of the challenges ahead in Japan.

Political Situation After the Fukushima Nuclear Disaster

Already three years have passed since the shocking nuclear disaster at Fukushima. Severe accidents at the Fukushima Daiichi nuclear power station reignited public and political debates and led not only to a re-examination of and improvements in the institutional framework and nuclear safety regulation but also to the revisiting of national policy for using nuclear energy both at home and abroad. Furthermore, multifaceted risks of a systemic nature have been emerging and re-emerging in the social, political, and economic domains because the use of nuclear power in our country has been tightly and complexly interconnected with and interdependent on socioeconomic activities and has also produced nested or collective interests everywhere as a result of lock-in phenomena.

How, then, have the government and the utility companies dealt with these situations after the Fukushima accident?

In the aftermath of the accident, one investigation committee on the Fukushima nuclear power plant accident has been established after another.[8] All of four accident investigation reports were published by the middle of 2012 (RJIF2012, ICANPS2012, TEPCO2012, NAIIC2012). And the AESJ Committee (chaired by Prof. S. Tanaka) published its report in March, 2014 (AESJ2014). These investigation committees have

[8] Independent Commission (chaired by Prof. K. Kitazawa, April 2011), Government Committee (chaired by Prof. Y. Hatamura, May 2011), TEPCO's Commission (chaired by M. Yamazaki, June 2011), National Diet Commission (chaired by Prof. K. Kurokawa, December 2011)

drawn a wide range of lessons and challenges from technical, organizational and institutional points of view through technical data analysis, hearings, interviews, and their examinations.

In the light of strong public sentiment against nuclear power in the aftermath of the Fukushima nuclear crisis, of course, not only the general public also the nuclear fraternity had high expectations of sweeping change. However, both the Government and the Diet approved a reform of the nuclear safety regulatory bodies in June, 2012, that does not reflect the findings and recommendations of the National Diet Commission's final report.

As for the safety enhancement of nuclear facilities, the installation of costly hardware such as a large-scale seawall and filtered venting system according to a new retrofitting rule is now in progress without any comprehensive risk assessment of their effectiveness. Dr. S. Tanaka, Chairman of Nuclear Regulation Authority, says, "We will be tireless in our efforts to improve our regulatory measures so that Japan's nuclear regulation standards will be among the worlds highest".[9] And Dr. S. Matsuura, Chairman of the Japan Nuclear Safety Institute, on behalf of nuclear industry, also says, "We pursue the world's highest level of safety".[10] Needless to say, the utility companies are primarily responsible for safety through voluntary and continuous improvements. However, the societal perspectives and needs concerning nuclear safety have obviously changed somewhat. We should expand the horizon and take different contexts into consideration. It is important to more fully understand nuclear safety from broader societal perspectives rather than merely from a technological viewpoint. This is one of the major lessons learned from the Fukushima accident.

---

9 http://www.nsr.go.jp/english/e_nra/

10 http://www.genanshin.jp/english/association/establishment.html

Regarding the future nuclear energy policy, the Government by the then ruling Democratic Party of Japan established the Energy and Environment Council in the Cabinet Office in October, 2011, and adopted the Innovative Energy and Environment Strategy, including a nuclear phase-out scenario, after expert meetings, public hearings, and a poll in September, 2012. A few months later, however, Japanese energy policy once more changed following a dramatic win by the LDP at the general election in December, 2012.

The Abe government had not prepared itself for the new opportunities of dialogue and deliberation with stakeholders and citizens while some actors had radicalized their position. This has resulted in an increasing inability to conduct a rational dialogue, trapping our society in a vicious circle. There is no sign of the government organizing opportunities for inclusive dialogues even though public sentiment in the present situation is even becoming ambivalent to nuclear energy, perhaps because the gradually increasing adverse economic impact of the long-term shutdown of all of Japan's nuclear power plants is materializing. The Abe government has rather rapidly changed the nuclear policy instituted by the Democratic Party following the Fukushima nuclear disaster.

The role of the Atomic Energy Commission has been reviewed extensively in both the Noda and Abe governments, and nuclear policy-making and decision-making authority was then substantially transferred to the METI Agency of Natural Resources and Energy in June, 2014. Without any extensive discussion, nuclear power is now again positioned as a base-load power source in energy policy.

Anyway, organizational and administrative reforms of nuclear policy and safety regulation, enforcement of more rigid nuclear safety standards, and technical countermeasures have only been implemented in the last three years. And the National Diet has not yet considered any proposals by the Diet Investigation Commission.

The Fukushima onsite management strategy is not going as planned due to underlying logistical problems such as financing and the workforce, and the offsite decontamination program has been substantially delayed because of a deadlock over the siting of the interim storage of wastes such as contaminated soil. The Abe government seems to be lurching toward restarting nuclear power plants in the context of its growth strategy. Thus, the nuclear crisis and its political consequences are continuing. Both our society and the nuclear-related organizations have scarcely tackled the task of learning the essential lessons from the Fukushima disaster.

Many of the nuclear-related problems that we face can never be overcome technologically, but rather they are more likely to be solved by changing societal mechanisms to enable collaborative processes for, for example, generating knowledge making informed decisions. "The major risks are social," but they are still poorly understood. Prof. Granger Morgan says, "Risk is a highly interdisciplinary phenomenon and it takes an integrated view from all of the different perspectives to get things right".[11]

Risk Governance Process

The scope of risk governance is not restricted to the issue of risk alone, but embraces the justification of hazardous activities with the potential of becoming a major risk. Much of the time such justification is implicitly acknowledged, however, sometimes it is explicitly questioned by society.

---

11 IRGC 2003-2013 Interviews with IRGC Academics, pp 15-18, 2014

After the Fukushima nuclear disaster, justification of the use of nuclear energy has been explicitly questioned by the society. The Fukushima disaster occurred not only as a result of the failure of risk management by both TEPCO and regulatory bodies but also of a failure of governance.

The International Risk Governance Council defines risk governance as "the totality of actors, rules, conventions, processes and mechanisms concerned with how relevant risk information is collected, analyzed and communicated, and how management decisions are taken".[12]

Figure 1 shows the core of IRGC's risk governance framework (IRGC 2008). This consists of two parts. One is the assessment sphere on the right side, and other is the risk-handling sphere on the left side. The framework builds upon the logical structure of four phases called pre-assessment, appraisal, characterization and evaluation, and management. Communication plays the crucial role across all the phases.

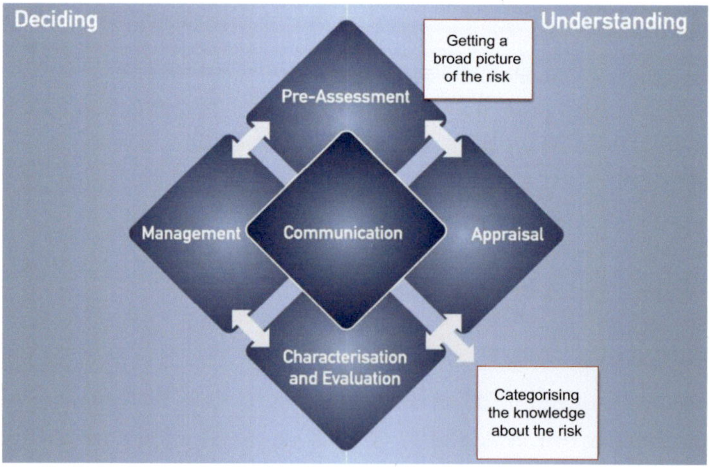

Figure 1: IRGC's risk governance process

---

12 IRGC, An Introduction to the IRGC Risk Governance Framework, 2008

Here, I focus on the assessment sphere, that is, knowledge generation and understanding, in relation to TA activity. Knowledge is needed to reduce complexity and uncertainty and to make ambiguity comprehensible. Understanding is also equally important. If knowledge exists but is not understood by decision makers, stakeholders, and the public, then risk governance becomes highly vulnerable.

One of the distinctive features of this risk governance framework is the pre-assessment phase that consists of problem framing, early warning, screening, and scientific conventions. This task clarifies the various perspectives on a risk, defines the issue to be looked at, and forms the baseline for how a risk is assessed and managed.

Socially problematic issues are "invisible risks". A typical example would be BSE. We never look at this sort of risk unless you are ready to look at what is going on. In the case of risks with long-term latency or a creeping nature, it is essential whether or not one tries to look out for signals that are physical, verbal, or nonverbal in nature. For those who wish to conceal invisible risks, the start of risk appraisal may become fatal, and thus a main battlefield will move upstream of risk appraisal. Examples are: When, where, how, and by whom should the task of framing be carried out, and what sorts of problems and why should we label issues as risk problems. The determination of the 5W1H of pre-assessment is therefore crucial and a truly societal issue.

Risk appraisal is composed of both a scientific risk assessment and an assessment of concern. The implementation of concern assessment is also a distinctive feature of this governance framework. Social scientists should play a key role in this task. What are the public's concerns and perceptions? What is the social response to the risk? Is there a possibility of political mobilization or potential conflict? What role do existing institutions, governance structures, and the media play in defining public concerns?

Evidence-based risk characterization generates knowledge for making the necessary judgment on the tolerability or acceptability, or both, of a risk and for balanced policy making. The evidence collected and summarized here goes beyond the classic natural scientific knowledge reservoir and includes economic and social science expertise. In the course of risk characterization, scientists are asked to design a multicriteria profile of the risk in question, make a judgment about the seriousness of the risk, and suggest potential options to deal with the risk.

Role of Technology Assessment in Nuclear Risk Governance

The I2TA project[13] conducted by the University of Tokyo defines TA as the "institutions and practices which support problem-definition (agenda setting) or decision-making for the development of technology and society by anticipating societal impacts of emerging technologies that are difficult to be governed by conventional research, innovation and legal systems at an early stage of the technology development" [14]. According to this working definition, TA activities can play two roles in the risk governance process.

First, TA is able to basically fulfill the functions of framing problems and setting agendas, which are key roles of the pre-assessment task in the risk governance process, and get a broad picture of the potential of the technology concerned. Limited-scope TA has the function of bringing

[13] This is the acronym for the project Innovation and Institutionalization of Technology Assessment. See http://i2ta.org/english/english.html.

[14] http://i2ta.org/files/RS-SCJ_20080922.pdf

up societal issues and provides input to the societal discussion about the 5W1H of pre-assessment. An important factor in limited-scope TA activity is stakeholder engagement.

Second, full-scope TA activity is knowledge generation itself in the risk governance process. Scientific evidence of the multifaceted societal impact derived by risk appraisal and characterization by an interdisciplinary team of experts, that is, information providing a complete picture of what is known about risk and what is and may remain unknown, helps reach an informed societal judgment for managing risks of technology. The success of full-scope TA activity relies heavily on interdisciplinary collaboration.

The tasks of risk governance should be continuous, so TA activities also should be done continuously at an appropriate stage of technology development, and timely on the occasion of the discovery of relevant scientific knowledge or of changes in the socioeconomic-political context, or of both. It would lead to societal learning and adaptive risk management.

Technology Assessment Today in Japan

In the Symposium on the Openness of Science and Technology Policy Processes held at the University of Tokyo in March, 2010, it was emphasized that TA is a tool supporting decision making that makes it possible to visualize the multifaceted impact of the technology concerned.[15] In the 4th Science and Technology Basic Plan (2011–2015),[16] the Japanese government noted the reinforcement of the following points: first is to examine what TA should really be, second is to promote TA activities about emerging technologies associated with bio-

15 http://i2ta.org/files/L-all.pdf (in Japanese)
16 http://www8.cao.go.jp/cstp/kihonkeikaku/index4.html (in Japanese)

ethical issues, third is to develop activities to share the outcomes of TA with the public, and fourth is to exploit TA for building a broader consensus about improving nuclear safety.

However, these steps have not yet been initiated. There is no sign that the government will have TA conducted for nuclear energy in the new socio economic-political context, although the Atomic Energy Commission pointed out the importance of TA in its statement dated December, 2012.17 In addition, it seems that awareness of the benefits of TA is declining in discussions about the 5th Science and Technology Plan.

In Japan, as a science and technology nation, the awareness and understanding of TA among politicians, policy makers, scientists, and engineers as a whole are really insufficient and have hardly been altered even though Japan is a dynamically changing society. While promoting science, technology, and innovation policy as the growth strategy of the Abe government, the practical use of TA is not explicitly ranked as a prerequisite of R&D of an emerging technology. One of underlying problems that TA activities do not pervade throughout the science and technology policy arena may be that politicians and policy makers in our country are apt to make light of the assessment/evaluation activity while attaching great importance to discovery and production.

Challenges Ahead in Japan

The social trust toward nuclear energy has been seriously eroded in Japan. Before the Fukushima disaster, nuclear energy stakeholders had lacked an understanding for slow-moving societal changes and for citizens' concerns and interests and many deficits can be observed in the

---

17 http://www.aec.go.jp/jicst/NC/about/kettei/121225-1_e.pdf

risk governance process. Since Fukushima, a few deficits have been slightly corrected, but critical deficits continue in the status quo. It even seems that some deficits are getting worse (see the appendix).

First, full-scope TA of nuclear energy is urgently needed to show the multifaceted societal impact and risk profile in order to provide legitimacy and restore trust. Second, the Council for Science and Technology Policy (CSTP) has adopted the Impulsing Paradigm Change through Disruptive Technologies (ImPACT) program.[18] The aim of ImPACT is to create the disruptive innovation that, if realized, will bring about major changes in the state of industry and society and to promote high-risk high-impact R&D. Five such themes have been identified. It is important to consider the obligation of TA to examine the technology candidates in the ImPACT program.

TA is a manner of a science and technology nation. Third, interdisciplinary communication and collaboration among social scientists and engineering professionals pose a big challenge. TA does not belong only to scientists and engineers. They have a role, but so do social scientists such as sociologists. Sociological insights are necessary inputs to determining policy for science, technology, and innovation. It seems, however, that technology is of no concern to Japanese sociologists as a whole and thus they are not very aware of TA activities, although the study of science, technology, and society (STS) in Japan has steadily developed in the past decade.

Finally, the development and implementation of educational programs on TA at universities also constitute a big challenge in Japan. Since 2010 the University of Tokyo has provided practical education in technology assessment at the Graduate School of Public Policy, as shown in

18 http://www8.cao.go.jp/cstp/sentan/kakushintekikenkyu/basicpolicy.pdf

Table 1. The aim of the lecture is to better understand TA in the context of public policy through case studies of emerging technologies. Participants are graduate students from Public Policy, Engineering, Science, Law and Politics, Interdisciplinary Information Studies, Medicine, and the Arts and Sciences.

Table 1: Overview of the educational program on TA

Contents during one semester (3 h/week * 14 weeks)	Lectures providing an overview of TA (history, overseas situation, methodology) Lectures on technologies subject to TA by experts (professors of UTokyo) Group works of TA (investigations, interviews, group discussions) Production of a TA report for a specific addressee Presentations of TA results
Topics	2014: VR and AR technologies, Space debris removal technology 2010–13: Brain–machine interface, Self-driving car, Large-scale simulation technology, M2M, Regenerative medicine (cornea), Geo-engineering technology, Smart grid system (smart meter), Large-scale offshore wind farm, Partitioning & transmutation technology for MAs and LLFPs, Fuel cell vehicle, Deep ocean water utilization technology, etc.

Concluding Remarks

Facing the unprecedented nuclear disaster, the words "unexpected" and "unforeseeable" flew about among diverse stakeholders. As mentioned before, these gaps in perception gave rise to societal risk issues of high complexity and ambiguity that may be hard to deal with. It is important to make an effort to reduce the number and impact of unexpected and/or unforeseeable consequences before the occurrence of an adverse event. A good understanding of risk cascading and its impact, accompanied by the Fukushima nuclear disaster, certainly provides us with many valuable implications for building a secure and resilient nation.

TA could end up reducing the societal costs of introducing new technology into our society, so we need to think in terms of anticipating what could occur and, very importantly, of creating feedback on this anticipation for the ongoing decision-making and policy processes.

References

Rebuild Japan Initiative Foundation: Investigation and Verification Report on the Fukushima Nuclear Power Station Accident, March 2012 (Japanese)

Tokyo Electric Power Co., Inc. (TEPCO): Fukushima Nuclear Accident Analysis Report, June 2012.

The Japanese Government: Final Report by TEPCO Fukushima Nuclear Power Station Accident Investigation and Verification Committee, June 2012 (Japanese).

The National Diet of Japan: The Official Report of the Fukushima Nuclear Accident Independent Investigation Commission, July 2012.

From Intermediary to Intermedia: Technology Assessment (TA) and Responsible Research and Innovation (RRI)

Go Yoshizawa

Three Years After …

In the afternoon of March 11, 2011, the RISTEX-funded project Innovation and Institutionalization of Technology Assessment in Japan (i2TA, 2007–2011) conducted a final public workshop in Roppongi, Tokyo. Within an hour of the start of the event, a strong earthquake suddenly rattled the old building and windows of the venue. Due to the number of aftershocks, the event was interrupted several times to evacuate participants.

This Great East Japan Earthquake and the consequent nuclear accident in Fukushima pushed policy makers to suspend the cabinet approval of the 4th Science and Technology Basic Plan, which was supposed to be released by the end of March, 2011, as a quinquennial plan for national science and technology policy (FY2012–2016). Five months later, the Cabinet Office finally approved the Plan with the addition of a set of policies for reconstruction, including a policy to 'promote technology assessment exercises on nuclear safety improvements in order to build a broad national consensus'.

What remains now three years after the end of the i2TA project and the start of the 4th Science and Technology Basic Plan? One of the main outputs of the i2TA project was the idea of 'third generation TA' (Yoshizawa, 2010), in which more collaborative, distributed governance is promoted. First, it would be good to now reconsider the the project's final evaluation in order to look back at this concept and examine the extent to which it has been put into practice.

Third Generation TA

To date, a variety of past TA activities and institutions have been categorized into two models, such as 'conventional' and 'new' (Smits, Leyten & Hertog, 1995) and 'instrumental' and 'discursive' (Petermann, 2000). These models correspond roughly to the first generation and the second generation of TA as illustrated in the following.

The first generation of TA (1G-TA) is symbolized by the US Congress Office of Technology Assessment (OTA), established in 1972. To conduct each exercise, the OTA set up an advisory committee consisting of a wide range of experts and stakeholders, and the OTA staff wrote a TA report utilizing issue networks with the committee members. Basically the OTA staff members, themselves experts, authored the report, the content of which is highly technical (Bimber, 1996; Whiteman, 1995).

In the 1970s, TA attempted to perform an early warning function – to forecast and diminish any negative future impact of technology at an early stage. In the 1980s, when it had been generally recognized that technology is inherently accompanied by uncertainty and unpredictability, TA became a means of strategic assessment, focusing on how technology can respond to political issues. In this generation, the whole issue network can be the addressee of TA products. However, the role of the TA was primarily to report to Congress. OTA was located in the Congress as the sponsor and the client of TA activities. 1G-TA can therefore be labeled as being parliament-centered (see Table 1).

The second generation of TA (2G-TA) is characterized by the focus on public debate and societal agenda-building, where the first generation tends to support policy making and decision making more directly. In this generation, it is not only experts who take a lead to complete the TA report; public participation has also been facilitated by the development of novel methods. This is particularly the case in the Netherlands and Denmark. Democracy guarantees the practice of a form of TA in which technology development is reconsidered through deliberation by selected citizens using their local knowledge. In other European countries, there are many TA exercises in which the concerned public is designated as the client or addressee. These exercises are often precautionary appraisals, a fact which invites the criticism that TA does not contribute to technological innovation. Since the late 1980s, 2G-TA has typically been based in European TA organizations. They are not only situated in parliaments (UK, France, Germany, and EU). Other implementing bodies include administrative organizations (Denmark) and science academies (Netherlands, Switzerland, Austria) (Shiroyama et al., 2009).

Participatory TA, as a key concept of 2G, essentially aims to make the assessment process more transparent and to encourage wider public debate and social learning (Joss & Bellucci, 2002). With a stronger emphasis on problem solving and participation, interactive TA stresses the importance of democracy by including all relevant stakeholders (Grin, van de Graaf & Hoppe, 1997). However, as it is a kind of social experiment carried out in a context as power-free as possible, interactive TA can neither replace nor fully play out these processes but rather it can influence them (Heiskanen, 2005). Either way, decision makers are likely to face a dilemma between a loss of legitimacy resulting from insufficient public participation and the possibility of endless debate among irreconcilable parties (Genus and Coles, 2005).

Now we come to the question of what constitutes the third generation of TA. This may entail a new form of governance. In network governance, participants themselves collectively govern the network as shared governance, or a sole network participant takes the role of leading the organization and governing the network. On the other hand, the network can be governed either by a mandate or by the members themselves with a network administrative organization (NAO). As a network broker coordinating and sustaining the network, the NAO may be a government entity or a nonprofit organization. As network members are called upon to collectively monitor the actions of the NAO leadership, trust across the network can be higher than lead organization governance (Provan & Kenis, 2008).

Distributed governance entails a process of the dispersion of power within and over a wide variety of actors and groups in the economy, society, and polity toward localized decision making, in which the best learning experience in a context of rapid change can be achieved by decentralized and flexible organizations (Paquet, 1997). In distributed governance, the NAO as a core organization of the governance of 3G-TA activities plays a more strategic role and becomes responsible for the distribution of actors and intelligence in the network. Whereas (network) governance often focuses only on human institutions, distributed governance also pays attention to information and knowledge activities, as designed in the theoretical framework of strategic intelligence (Kuhlmann et al., 1999). Therefore, the organization does not always simply utilize human and intellectual resources already distributed in the network, but often intentionally distributes them.

Whereas 2G-TA has undertaken communication and participatory exercises in a rather rough framework involving experts such as scientists and engineers as well as selected citizens, 3G-TA facilitates the active participation of intermediate actors between experts and the lay public, encompassing private manufacturers and retailers as intermediate consumers and users, workers, workers' unions, industrial and business associations, nonprofit organizations, consumer groups, local governments, social scientists, and journalists.

The legitimacy and credibility of TA practice is guaranteed, independent of the status of the participants or procedures such as their expertise or the democratic features that they intrinsically retain, but by societal verification on the basis of a process that is accountable to the public. Accordingly, the relevance of the process is to be examined by the participants themselves and revised constantly. The constituent participants, e.g., practitioners, sponsors, clients, and addressees, vary dynamically under the distributed governance.

The assessment aims not only to analyze the societal impact of technology at a point in time in the future, but also to intervene in the on-going research and development of technology on a real-time basis. In this way, TA "constructs" both the technology and the TA process itself. This double construction can be framed as a part of the transition management that foresees and shifts the sociotechnological paradigm and regime. This kind of TA, known as constructive TA, started in a minor way in the late 1980s and is now (together with real-time TA) quite visible (Rip, Misa & Schot, 1995; Guston & Sarewitz, 2002).

Moreover, there is another construction aspect in 3G-TA. As the i2TA project has demonstrated, such TA activities encourage the construction of institutions dedicated to TA by embedding the necessary functions into society. This can also be framed in the multilevel perspective of technological transitions (Genus & Coles, 2008).

Table 1: Three Generations of TA

	First Generation	Second Generation	Third Generation
Time	Since 1970s	Since 1990s	Since 2000s
Institutions	Parliament-centered (Government)	Parliament-related (Governance)	Collaborative (Distributed governance)
Key participants	Experts	Selected citizens and key stakeholders	Intermediate actors as well as the general public
Guarantee of legitimacy and credibility	Expertise	Democratic process	Societal verification
Approach	Early warning to Strategic	Precautionary to Constructive	Real-time and Communicative
Methods	Technical/Analytic	Social/Deliberative	Mixed (with information and network technologies)
Resources	Expert	Local	Existing

Remnant of (i2)TA

Apart from the deliberative poll introduced by the Democratic Party of Japan (DPJ) coalition government to stimulate public discussion on whether to withdraw from nuclear energy in 2012 (Mikami, 2014), the government has not yet performed any of the TA exercises on improving nuclear safety promised in the 4th Science and Technology Basic Plan.

What about the promises and our expectations? In i2TA, we proposed the following five options for the institutionalization of TA in Japan (i2TA, 2011):

(1) Diet (Japanese Parliament), as a supportive function for the research and analysis unit of the Select Committee on Science, Technology and Innovation in the House of Representatives;
(2) Government, as an independent TA unit under the Science, Technology and Innovation Strategy Headquarters, Cabinet Office;
(3) Science Council of Japan, assuring a wide range of practitioners in the Young Academy Committee through the enhancement of its administration. It could establish a TA unit;
(4) Governmental Funding Frame: (a) a policy to frame a certain proportion of the government R&D investment for TA activities engaging with a variety of research institutions, universities, and nonprofit organizations; or (b) under the frame of the "Science for Science, Technology and Innovation" and the "Science and Technology Communication" programs, or as a part of the Social Return Unit in a large-scale R&D program; and,
(5) R&D organizations, as a part of the unit for S&T diplomacy, science communication, and R&D strategy in the National Research and Development Organization integrating existing public R&D agencies.

Looking back over the last three years, only one TA institution has been substantiated. This institution accords with option (4b) and is left as a sign of hope for 3G-TA where there is room for TA researchers and practitioners to exchange their knowledge and create a network of TA-like activities through the "Science for RE-designing Science, Technology and Innovation Policy (SciREX)" program.

At a grass-roots level, in September 2010, some of the i2TA project members set up as the successor body to i2TA, the Technology Assessment Research Demonstration Project in the Policy Alternative Research Institute (PARI) of the University of Tokyo. As a top-down initiative, in August, 2014, the National Graduate School for Policy Studies (GRIPS) established the Science, Technology and Innovation Policy Research Center under the frame of the SciREX program.

These institutions are supposed to perform as a kind of intermediary providing a link between knowledge and policy, like parliamentary TA organizations in Europe, through which TA exercises are conducted and performed. However, when it becomes more difficult for such intermediaries to survive in the modern sociopolitical context, as in the cases of the Danish Board of Technology (Horst, 2014) and the Flemish TA organizations (van Oudheusden & Yoshizawa, 2013), we may need to rethink the role of intermediaries in embedding TA functions in society.

Rethinking the Role of Intermediaries

There have been serious entangled academic discussions in the study of intermediaries, covering at least three concepts of 'intermediary'. First, there are familiar discussions on the linkage between knowledge and the market or society in innovation and technology management studies, namely organizations which have been called 'third parties', 'knowledge brokers', and 'boundary organizations' to name a few (Howells, 2006).

Secondly, some discussions focus on the intermediate agency in the financial flow from government agencies to research bodies as typified as Japanese public funding agencies, often found in the study of research policy (IFENG, 2011).

Corresponding to this, thirdly, there is an extensive literature in evaluation studies focusing on the agencies dedicated to program management as the middle level of intervention, while assuming a stratified structure of policy, program, and project in the public intervention in research and innovation – though the stratification is often loose when various scholars do not differentiate between project and program in management studies (Artto *et al.*, 2009) and program and policy evaluation studies (e.g. Chen, 2005). In brief, discussions about organizations intermediate between (1) knowledge producers and market or society as knowledge users, (2) funders and beneficiaries, or (3) policy makers and project teams become intermingled between research and innovation studies, economics, science and technology studies, policy and evaluation studies, and organization and management studies. Given this, a working definition of intermediary is "an organization linking a sponsor/client and a producer/addressee, in order to produce, transfer, exchange or use knowledge for social public values" (Yoshizawa & Nishimura, 2013).

It might be useful here to focus on boundary organizations as the most familiar concept of intermediary in science, technology, and society (STS) studies and public policy studies. The very simple understanding of boundary organizations (Guston, 1999, 2001; Cash, 2001) can be summarized in the following three essential points:

(1) participation by researchers and policy makers;
(2) coproduction of 'boundary objects'; and
(3) accountability to both the research and policy communities

As some say (O'Mahony & Bechky, 2008), the durable nature of boundary organizations serves as a catalyst for delineating interests. However, in Japan and possibly in other countries as well, boundary organizations are always vulnerable. The reason is closely related to the reason why

TA has never become institutionalized in Japan over the last forty years. First of all, there is a general public distrust of intermediaries. There must be a holistic commitment to the intermediary from each standpoint.

In particular, the research community tends to be closed and exclusive while asking community members to fully commit to research and other community activities and thus spreading the them-or-us mind-set. Furthermore, there is an implicit requirement of a reduction in the cost of the transaction from knowledge to policy. Although Japan is not a very technocratic society, the policy community usually follows the research community, reflecting the politics of consultation (Schwartz, 1998). Through a great number of policy advisory councils in individual government ministries and agencies, prominent researchers can be content to directly participate in the policy process, as if they independently exercised power and authority. However, policy makers often keep them under control.

It appears that there is also organizational distrust of intermediaries from research communities in Japan. The governance of the research community has undergone little change during the past century, and this can be the real villain behind the unsuccessful history of the establishment of intermediaries including TA organizations. Japanese academic societies originally emerged and evolved with the establishment of a national university to nurture technocrats and its alumni reunions in the nineteenth century. Although mostly funded and supported by public money, researchers have since been free from accountability and responsibility to society while also expecting respect of their academic autonomy. As a consequence, they have retained much power and influence over legislative and administrative bodies and are consequently likely to devalue intermediaries.

One important question on the concept of intermediaries is the relationship between structure and agency, or the organization and individual. In the dynamic field of exchanging knowledge, individuals are no longer associated with a single organization. They constitute essential actors in interorganizational networks and collaboration by means of organizational improvisation and communities of practice. Surely 3G-TA can pose one attempt to broaden and open up TA (Ely, van Zwanenberg & Stirling, 2014), but I would rather emphasize three key figures towards more agent-based thinking.

As emphasised elsewhere (Yoshizawa, 2012), individual cognition, connections, and commitments are fundamental in the dynamic and sustainable management of a malleable and vulnerable intermediary responsive to situations, contexts, and environments.

Intermedia for TA and RRI

Just as intermediary usually implies an organization in policy and management studies, this paper introduces the new term 'intermedia' as the media between agents to produce, transfer, exchange or use knowledge for social public values. The media do not only refer to intermediate organizations and individuals, but also to networks, communities, spaces, and mass media as well as to ambience and atmosphere.

A conventional governance perspective is formalized, static, and restricted to organizational processes and networks, the decision-making in which is based on either libertarian individuals or authoritarian society. In the Japanese context, however, as represented by terms like *seken* (world-between) and *kuuki* (air), people often never make a clear decision on an issue but rather deal with it in a tacit, ad hoc, and peer-pressured manner. Such intangible ambient media can also perform as intermedia. This is particularly important when we need to go beyond discussions on responsibility in research products or processes. Tidd and Bessant (2009) suggest another two core dimensions: "position innovation," i.e., changes in the context in which the products/services are introduced, and "paradigm innovation," i.e., changes in the underlying mental models which frame what the organization does. These two dimensions are the most novel and interesting types of innovation (Rowley, Baregheh & Sambrook, 2011), but it may be more difficult for someone to take responsibility for such intangible and unspecific activities.

Changes in the context and the underlying mental models are far from easy. First of all, we may need to change our conventional mental models of the nexus between science and society, neither going to a positivist or technocratic end in which science linearly serves society, nor going to a constructivist or relativistic end in which science and society are indistinguishably coproduced with each other. It is tricky in that positivism is clothed even in a constructivist term like trans-science.

Alvin Weinberg, one of the ancestors in science and technology studies, defined trans-scientific as for "questions which can be asked of science and yet which cannot be answered by science" (Weinberg, 1972: 209, emphasis in the original). In literal terms, the askers are always in society, and science always stands on the answerers' side. This asymmetric configuration can be more obvious in the practice of responsible research and innovation (RRI). In conventional discussions of the social responsibility of scientists, it is supposed that individual consequentialist moral scientists execute a social contract and perform their accountability to the whole of society. This one-to-many relation, however, seems to be quite the opposite in reality. A great number of anonymous individuals spread throughout society can collectively rush to the world of science at once and ask (or attack at times) a few named scientists.

At this stage, the targeted actors are not just the individual scientists but rather the science community as a whole, simply and unfortunately because most of the members of society are unaware and uninformed as to how the science community works and how there can be collaboration and conflict between different science tribes in disciplines, laboratories, schools, institutions, regions and nations under the name of science. Although an analogy to something serious that is happening in military affairs may not be very smart, this conflict between scientists and citizens can be seen as a kind of asymmetric warfare (cf. Hardt & Negri 2002).

Under these circumstances, individual scientists find it hard to retain a Janus-faced responsibility – as an expert exhibiting scientific accountability on the one hand, and as a citizen showing general moral responsibility to the public. It may be better that they remain scientific experts, but even more as 'experts who take a step forward' for society (RISTEX, 2013). Showing considerable responsibility and responsiveness to society often exhausts scientists. Citizens may also have to improve their institutional perspective (rather than scientific literacy) in order to communicate better with the science community. To moderate scientists' responsiveness and weaken responsibility to the public, intermedia should play a critical mediating role.

The Age of Intermedia

One of the remaining agenda items is on how to dissolve or mitigate the asymmetric (epistemic) relationship between science and society. Open science may be a possible solution in the sense that citizens can participate in science and recognize how science works not only in nature but also in the scientific community. We can also expect public engagement to be a key for the dissolution. However, public involvement has recently been criticized in terms of under-utilization in the policy-making process (Rogers-Hayden & Pidgeon, 2007; van Oudheusden, 2011; Rask, 2013).

Apart from utility in policy, the engaged public is nonetheless unlikely to change its mind and understanding of the scientific community, if not of science itself. Public involvement seems to follow the same track of process innovation, in the sense that both believe that process change may bring good results for policy or the market regardless of the context (position) or the actors' mental models (paradigm).

The responsible conduct of research (RCR) may have similar pitfalls, but it is strategically more feasible and reasonable to highlight this concept and practice as an entry point for good governance in research communities. Unlike public involvement, which is more focused on the nexus between public and government for policy making than the one between public and science, RCR is directed to science and focused on the reform of research communities. Keys to open up ways from RCR to RRI in Japan include working with research managers and administrators and, thereby, reform of universities and academic societies. The forty years of silence for the institutionalization of TA in Japan could be changed and a new history will come with the destruction of the ancient regime for research communities and structures.

References

Artto, K, Martinsuo, M., Gemünden, H.G. & Murtoaro, J. (2009). "Foundations of program management: A bibliometric view", International Journal of Project Management, 27(1): 1–18.

Bimber, B. (1996) The Politics of Expertise in Congress: The Rise and Fall of the Office of Technology Assessment. New York: State University of New York Press.

Cash, D.W. 2001. "'In order to aid in diffusion useful and practical information': agricultural extension and boundary organizations", *Science, Technology and Human Values* 26(4): 431–453.

Chen, H-T. (2005) Practical Program Evaluation: Assessing and Improving Planning, Implementation, and Effectiveness. Sage.

Ely, A., van Zwanenberg, P. & Stirling, A. (2014) "Broadening out and opening up technology assessment: approaches to enhance international development, co-ordination and democratisation", *Research Policy* 43(3): 505–518.

Genus, A. & Coles, A.-M. (2005) "On constructive technology assessment and limitations on public participation in technology assessment", Technology Analysis & Strategic Management 17(4): 433–443.

Genus, A. & Coles, A.-M. (2008) "Rethinking the multi-level perspective of technological transitions", Research Policy 37(9): 1436–1445.

Grin, J., van de Graaf, H. & Hoppe, R. (1997) *Technology Assessment through Interaction: A Guide*. Working Document, vol. 57. The Hague: Rathenau Institute.

Guston, D.H. (1999) "Stabilizing the boundary between US politics and science: the role of the Office of Technology Transfer as a boundary organization", *Social Studies of Science* 29(1): 87–111.

Guston, D.H., ed. (2001) "Boundary organizations in environmental policy and science", special issue on *Science, Technology and Human Values* 26(4).

Guston, D.H. & Sarewitz, D. (2002) "Real-time technology assessment", *Technology in Society* 24(1–2): 93–109.

Hardt, M. & Negri, A. (2004) Multitude: War and Democracy in the Age of Empire. Penguin Press.

Heiskanen, E. (2005) "Taming the Golem – an experiment in participatory and constructive technology assessment", *Science Studies* 18(1): 52–74.

Horst, M. (2014) "On the weakness of strong ties", *Public Understanding of Science* 23(1): 43–47.

Howells, J. (2006) "Intermediation and the role of intermediaries in innovation", *Research Policy*, 35(5): 715–728.

IFENG (Institute for Future Engineering). (2011) Analysis Report of R&D Systems in Overseas Governmental R&D Institutes [in Japanese].

i2TA (Innovation and Institutionalization of Technology Assessment in Japan). (2011) 'What is the relevance of TA?', 31 March 2011. Available at http://i2ta.org/files/TA_en_20110331.pdf

Joss, S. & Bellucci, S., eds. (2002) Participatory Technology Assessment: European Perspectives. London: Centre for the Study of Democracy.

Kuhlmann, S. et al. (1999) *Improving Distributed Intelligence in Complex Innovation Systems*. Final report of the Advanced Science & Technology Policy Planning Network (ASTPP). Karlsruhe.

Mikami, N. (2014) "Public participation and deliberation about nuclear energy policy: a case study of 'national debate' after Fukushima Accident", presented at XVIII ISA Word Congress of Sociology, Yokohama, 15 July 2014.

O'Mahony, S. & Bechky, B.A. (2008) "Boundary organizations: enabling collaboration among unexpected allies", *Administrative Science Quarterly* 53(3): 422–459.

Paquet, G. (1997) "States, communities and markets: the distributed governance scenario", pp. 25–46 in T.J. Courchene, ed., *The Nation State in a Global Information Era: Policy Challenges*. Kingston: John Deustch Institute for the Study of Economic Policy.

Petermann, T. (2000) "Technology assessment units in the European parliamentary systems", pp. 37–61 in N. J. Vig and H. Paschen, eds., *Parliaments and Technology*. New York: State University of New York Press.

Provan, K.G. & Kenis, P. (2008) "Modes of network governance: structure, management, and effectiveness", *Journal of Public Administration Research and Theory* 18(2): 229–252.

Rask, M. (2013) "The tragedy of citizen deliberation – two cases of participatory technology assessment", *Technology Analysis & Strategic Management* 25(1): 39–55.

RISTEX (Research Institute of Science and Technology for Society). (2013) *Expanding the Range of Participants and a New Role for Experts: Interaction between Science, Technology and Society*. Report of R&D Focus Area: Science, Technology and Humanity. Available at http://www. ristex.jp/result/science/pdf/20131128_2.pdf

Rip, A., Misa, T.J. & Schot, J., eds. (1995) *Managing Technology in Society: The Approach of Constructive Technology Assessment*. London and New York: Pinter Publishers.

Rogers-Hayden, T. & Pidgeon, N. (2007) "Moving engagement 'upstream'? Nanotechnologies and the Royal Society and Royal Academy of Engineering's inquiry", *Public Understanding of Science* 16(3): 345–364.

Rowley, J., Baregheh, A. & Sambrook, S. (2011) "Towards an innovative-type mapping tool", *Management Decision* 49(1): 73-86.

Schwartz, F. (1998) Advice and Consent: The Politics of Consultation in Japan. Cambridge University Press.

Shiroyama, H., Yoshizawa, G., Matsuo, M. & Suzuki, T. (2009) "Institutional options and operational issues in Technology Assessment:

lessons from experiences in the United States and Europe", *IEEE Conference Proceedings for 2009 Atlanta Conference on Science and Innovation Policy*, 2–3 Oct 2009.

Smits, R., Leyten, J. & Hertog, P.D. (1995) "Technology assessment and technology policy in Europe: new concepts, new goals, new infrastructures", *Policy Sciences* 28(3): 271–299.

Tidd, J. & Bessant, J. (2009) Managing Innovation: Integrating Technological, market and Organizational Change. Chichester, John Wiley & Sons, Ltd.

van Oudheusden, M. (2011) "Questioning 'participation': a critical appraisal of its conceptualization in a Flemish participatory technology assessment", *Science and Engineering Ethics* 17(4): 673–690.

van Oudheusden, M. & Yoshizawa, G. (2013) "Governance in Japan and Belgium: building on experiments with Technology Assessment and TA-like activities", presented at Asia-Pacific Science, Technology & Society Network Conference, Singapore, 15 July 2013.

Weinberg, A. (1972) "Science and trans-science", *Minerva* 10(2): 209–222.

Whiteman, D. (1995) Communication in Congress: Members, Staff, and the Search for Information. University Press of Kansas.

Yoshizawa, G. (2010) "Third generation of technology assessment", presented at Annual Meeting of the Society for the Social Studies of Science (4S), Tokyo, 28 August 2010.

Yoshizawa, G. (2012) "Anticipatory and participatory governance: revisiting technology assessment on nuclear energy in Japan", *Journal of Disaster Research* 7(Sp): 511–516.

Yoshizawa, G. & Nishimura, Y. (2013) "The role of intermediaries linking knowledge and public and social values", *IAMOT 2013 Proceedings*, 14–18 April 2013.

Parliamentary TA: Lessons to Be Learned from the Established

Constanze Scherz and Christina Merz

Introduction

Technology assessment (TA) serves several functions in several contexts. It is a concept of interdisciplinary (and increasingly also transdisciplinary) research. Furthermore, TA can be regarded as problem-oriented research and is therefore predestined to support policy makers by understanding the problems connected to the social-technical challenges of our time. By performing this function, the aim should be to assess the available options for managing them. But the question is: What are triggers and barriers to reaching this goal?

In the following we refer to TA as a policy-consulting method in the field of parliamentary TA. First we ask how the institutionalization of parliamentary TA has taken place. In which countries and under which political and societal conditions have TA institutions been established? Afterwards we can clearly demonstrate the heterogeneity of the established TA institutions: they follow different organizational models and types of association to parliament. Some of their histories can be told as successful stories, while others have failed and been closed.

At a time when numerous initiatives all over the world are trying to institutionalize TA at a (national) parliament for the first time, it is also worth focusing on the established. The reasons are manifold. As role models, the established institutions should time and again reflect on their own legitimacy and their current tasks. Are the formats they follow still sufficient to provide advice on time and appropriately regarding the complexities of our contemporary societies? This kind of reflection is not only helpful but a necessary condition for persisting. In the final section we will therefore refer to some new developments, formats, and networking activities, some of which have already started. They indicate that the established parliamentary TA institutions have already learned some of their lessons.

Institutionalization in the US and Europe[19]

The Cradle of TA: The Office of Technology Assessment

Concepts of TA were already discussed in the United States in the late 1960s "when tensions flared between executive and the congressional branches of the federal government about access to technical and scientific advice" (Sadowski/Guston 2015:53). After years of debate about the conceivable methods and styles of advice, Congress created the Office of Technology Assessment (OTA) in 1972 in order to assist and support the legislative "in the identification and consideration of existing and probable impacts of technological application [to ensure that] the consequences of technological applications be anticipated, understood, and considered in determination of public policy on existing and emerging national problems" (Blair 2013: Appendix).

OTA was the first and largest parliamentary TA office, and its history has therefore often been studied (e.g., Bimber 1996, Guston 2003,

[19] Parts of the sub-chapters 1 and 2 were published in the journal *Filosofija nauki i tehniki* (Philosophy of Science and Technology), Russian Academy of Sciences, 2015, in review.

Keiper 2004). OTA's original design was to provide a kind of "early warning" for the Congress on the potential impact of new and emerging kinds of technology. The first report addressed the viability of generic drugs.[20] This report also included explicit policy recommendations, which was discontinued in the following reports due to "[…] the OTA legislation that required that assessment reports […] be approved by an affirming majority vote […]" (Blair 2013:451) of OTA's Board, which was composed of Republican as well as Democratic members of the Congress. And this was not the only challenge OTA had to face. Among the studies, papers, and reports that OTA provided were a large number of comprehensive technology assessments "[…] which it produced and delivered to congressional committees upon formal request" (Sadowski 2015:15). For this purpose, it established a detailed and extensive process to be able to include a variety of stakeholder perspectives on the specific topic of interest (see for example Blair 2013:452 et seq.).

However, this attempt to include different opinions and thus provide neutral results to the Congress was not only a challenge in regard to the particular studies and assessments but also for OTA's self-perception and inner organization. The somehow ambivalent position in being an institution close to the legislative and having the Congress as main client on the one hand while on the other trying to establish itself as a neutral, somehow independent, institution led to processes of self-reflection.

These processes were also accompanied by changes in OTA's leadership, and the different directors – the one more, the other less – stimulated self-studying of OTA's work and the methods used when carrying out a TA study (see for example Guston 2001). In this sense, at least the inner-organizational structure of OTA was never fully established before OTA

20 OTA – Office of Technology Assessment (1974): Drug Bioequivalence, NTIS order #PB-244862, July 1974. Washington, DC; https://www.princeton.edu/~ota/disk3/1974/7401/7401.PDF

had to close its doors in 1995 after more than 20 years of operation. And when thinking about these attempts to handle the ambivalent situation of being neutral and having the Congress as its main client, it is a kind of irony of fate that OTA fell victim to political leadership. Although, on the other hand, one must admit that the neutral position and self-perception of OTA was judged ambivalently (see for example Bimber 1996) and Sadowski (2015:17) regards OTA as probably being "a challenger" to Republican goals and its closure as a response to it, in the end, the reasons for OTA's closing are not fully clear. Blair (2013:453), for example, points to OTA's processes of self-perception when he mentions, among other reasons, "[…] the lack of a mission fully integrated with a well-established congressional process […]".

Whatever the reasons that were attributed, there seems to be a consensus that OTA was an easy victim in times when the "Contract with America" was not only a big promise in regard to its content but also one that was directly linked to the pledge of implementing the promised reforms within 100 days. In this sense, the consolidation of the federal budget as one important campaign pledge of the Republicans and the Contract with America had cost OTA its right to exist. Interestingly, Guston (2001:11) comments on the closure of OTA as follows: "It is unclear whether it is necessary to agree on why OTA passed in order to agree on what, if anything, should replace it."

Parliamentary TA in Europe: The Established Institutions as Heterogeneous Role Models

Whatever the lessons learned from the closure of OTA, the OTA served and still serves as a role model for others. Indeed, the same approach to institutionalize TA pursued in the United States was taken up by European parliamentary TA institutions founded in the 1980s and 1990s. But what does this really mean for the institutionalization of TA in Europe or beyond? Indeed, several terms are often used when TA is described from the perspective of countries in which TA's role as a consultant and advisor on policy is regarded as settled. Even in the introduction of this article, we have used different adjectives, such as established, institutionalized, and organized, in an indistinct manner. However, when trying to talk explicitly about the institutionalization of TA in this section, we must first of all clarify what we are talking about or at least indicate what we are not talking about. In the following, we will write about institutionalized TA in the sense of parliamentary TA.

Though this term often leads to the conclusion that TA is directly included or connected to a parliament, it is important to notice that there are indeed several forms as to how parliamentary TA is performed within European countries and that these forms also differ from the OTA model in many respects, e.g., organizationally as well as with regard to their methodologies and mission (e.g., Vig/Paschen 2000). In 2012 Ganzevles and van Est published a paper in the course of the EU-funded project Parliaments and Civil Society in Technology Assessment (PACITA)[21] about TA practices in Europe.

The authors point out in detail that "[...] one should be careful when equating or identifying performing Parliamentary TA with a Parliamentary TA organisation. We therefore prefer to talk about a TA organisation that has the task to perform Parliamentary TA, possibly amongst performing other tasks" (Ganzevles/van Est 2012:21). And not only this, Ganzevles and van Est distinguish five organizational types of parliamentary TA practice that are currently operational (2012:13-14):

21 http://www.pacitaproject.eu/

- Model 1 reflects mainly parliamentary involvement (Finland,[22] France,[23] Greece,[24], Italy[25])
- Model 2 reflects a shared parliament-science involvement (Catalonia (Spain),[26] European Union,[27] Germany,[28] the UK,[29] and the USA[30] (until 1995)
- Model 3 entails a shared parliament-science-society involvement (Flanders (Belgium until 2012[31]), Denmark (as of 2012)[32])
- Model 4 reflects a shared science-government involvement (Austria[33])
- Model 5 reflects a shared involvement of all four spheres: parliament-government-science-society (the Netherlands,[34] Norway,[35] Switzerland,[36] USA (for the GOA)[37])

---

22 The Committee for the Future, Finland; see http://web.eduskunta.fi/Resource.phx/parliament/committees/future.htx?lng=en

23 L'Office parlementaire d'évaluation des choix scientifiques et technologiques (OPECST), France; see http://www.assemblee-nationale.fr/commissions/opecst-index.asp

24 Greek Permanent Committee of Technology Assessment (GPCTA), Greek; see http://www.oeaw.ac.at/ita/fileadmin/epta/countryreport/greece.html

25 Comitato per la Valutazione delle Scelte Scientifiche e Tecnologiche (VAST), Italy; see http://vast.camera.it/

26 El Consell Assessor del Parlament sobre Ciència i Tecnologia (CAPCIT), Catalonia (Spain); see http://www.parlament.cat/web/composicio/capcit

27 Science and Technology Options Assessment (STOA), European Union; see http://www.europarl.europa.eu/stoa/

28 Office of Technology Assessment at the German Bundestag (TAB), Germany; see http://www.tab-beim-bundestag.de/en/index.html

29 Parliamentary Office of Science and Technology (POST), UK; see http://www.parliament.uk/mps-lords-and-offices/offices/bicameral/post/

30 Office of Technology Assessment (OTA); USA, see http://ota.fas.org/ (Archive)

31 Instituut Samenleving en Technologie (IST), Flanders (Belgium), see http://www.oeaw.ac.at/ita/fileadmin/epta/countryreport/flanders.html

32 Danish Board of Technology (DBT), Denmark; see http://www.oeaw.ac.at/ita/fileadmin/epta/countryreport/denmark.html

33 Institute of Technology Assessment (ITA), Austria, see http://www.oeaw.ac.at/ita/en/home

34 Rathenau Instituut, Netherlands, see http://www.rathenau.nl/en.html

This differentiation demonstrates that Parliamentary TA "[…] is modeled as an activity at the interplay between parliament, government, science and society" (Ganzevles/van Est 2012:15). It is therefore important to consider that parliamentary TA has interlinkages to other societal institutions, or to express it in other words, parliamentary TA is always embedded in an "institutional environment" (Ganzevles/van Est 2012:18). And of course, this also influences the forms in which parliamentary TA is carried out and organized.

As the institutional environment is on the one hand context specific (for example, based on country-specific, cultural, political and societal differences) and on the other hand changes over time, actors wanting to establish TA within their countries should become clear about the multidimensional nature of parliamentary TA. Furthermore, when looking at the countries that already have institutionalized forms of parliamentary TA, the establishment of TA can be regarded as a process. In the beginning, every institution in Europe had its own preconditions with regard to, for example, the drivers, the sponsors, the proposed decision-making processes (with regard to, e.g., the theme selection), the proposed addressees, the proposed main function, and the planned time perspective. And as the history shows, especially the latter, the lifespan of the institutions that advise on politics, depends on the political system on the one hand and the political will on the other.

In dealing with these preconditions and by being captured in the existing "institutional environment" (Ganzevles/van Est 2012:18), every institution has had to undergo a process of learning or, even

35 Norwegian Board of Technology (NBT), Norway, see http://teknologiradet.no/english/

36 Centre for Technology Assessment TA-Swiss, Switzerland, see https://www.ta-swiss.ch/en/

37 U.S. Government Accountability Office (GAO), USA; see http://www.gao.gov/technology_assessment/key_reports

better, “institutional learning” (see Petermann/Scherz, 2005:283) where the organization had to learn to play its role, to develop its own structures, processes and rules. The organization figures out and at some point occupies “[…] the ‘manoeuvring space’ that [the particular] organisations [had] within their institutional context […]” (Ganzevles/van Est 2012:16). Therefore, the manner in which parliamentary TA was institutionalized and the national-specific processes that had to be undergone enable the respective “[…] TA organization to have an impact on the political debate” (Ganzevles/van Est 2012:19).

The Office of Technology Assessment at the German Bundestag: An Example for Establishing TA in a National Context

As a basis for reflection and in order to illustrate how the above-mentioned preconditions or processes looked in a specific case, in this section we will present the German example of TAB (the Office of Technology Assessment at the German Bundestag), which is operated by the Institute of Technology Assessment and Systems Analysis (ITAS at KIT). What were the reasons for institutionalizing TAB and, at the same time, for establishing TA in the political context in Germany?

TA at the German Bundestag is stable connected with TAB. Like in other European states, the idea of providing continuous technology assessment in support of parliament dates back to the 1970s. In that decade the debate on the opportunities and risks of scientific and technological developments increased. Numerous problematic consequences for society and the environment raised the awareness in the German Bundestag of the need for an early assessment and evaluation of the development and use of technology. The parliamentarians debated the opportunities, risks, and potentials of designing new forms of technology. And the discussion soon focused on the question of whether and how TA might be used in support of decision-making processes. Concerning the question of institutionalization, the debate gained momentum in 1973 with a motion by the (then opposition) Christian Democratic Union parliamentary group to establish an "Office for Evaluation of Technological Development at the German Bundestag".[38]

Numerous proposals from other parliamentary groups followed. In 1985 there was a joint decision by the parliamentary groups set up the "Study Commission on Assessment and Evaluation of Technological Impacts".[39] This Commission submitted a proposal on the "Institutionalization of an advisory body for technology assessment and evaluation at the German Bundestag" in 1986 and completed its work by the end of the electoral period with an interim report containing recommendations regarding the organization of technology assessment at the German Bundestag.[40]

Following the next federal elections, the next Bundestag again set up a Study Commission on TA. Its task was to adopt the criticism of the institutionalization model. In its final report, the Commission presented three different models for discussion and decision:

(4) The Christian Democratic Union and the Free Democratic Party suggested renaming the Committee on Research and Technology to "Committee on Research, Technology and Technology Assessment", which would be responsible for the initiation and political control of TA. An institution outside Parliament

38 See Bundestagsdrucksache 7/468, April 16, 1973; http://dipbt.bundestag.de/doc/btd/07/004/0700468.pdf (downloaded 2015-03-12)

39 See Bundestagsdrucksache 10/2937, February 27, 1985; http://dip21.bundestag.de/dip21/btd/10/029/1002937.pdf (downloaded 2015-03-12)

40 See Bundestagsdrucksache 10/5844, July 14, 1986; http://dip21.bundestag.de/dip21/btd/10/058/1005844.pdf (downloaded 2015-03-12)

would be commissioned to conduct TA studies and carry out "this task with a high degree of independence and responsibility" (Deutscher Bundestag 1989:14 et seq.).

(5) The Social Democratic Party proposed to establish a committee for parliamentary technology advice as well as a scientific unit (about 15 members) within the German Bundestag. The committee and the scientific unit should be supported by a "Board of Trustees" appointed by the German Bundestag (Deutscher Bundestag 1989:15 et seqq.).

(6) The Green Party voted for the establishment of a TA foundation which would be headed by members of the German Bundestag and non-parliamentary experts to be elected by the General Assembly of parliament. Furthermore, an institute would be assigned to the foundation, whose task would be to accompany TA studies and prepare them for the Parliament. Additionally, a permanent scientific unit would be attached to the Presidium of the German Bundestag, which would award TA studies to the foundation (Deutscher Bundestag 1989:17 et seqq.).

On November 16, 1989, the German Bundestag voted by majority of the Christian Democratic Union and the Free Democratic Party to rename the "Committee on Research and Technology" to "Committee on Research, Technology and Technology Assessment" and to authorize a scientific institution to conduct TA for the German Bundestag.[41] The German case shows that – despite their differences – all the parliamentary groups agreed on the need for a permanent TA institution "independent of elections and parliamentary cycles and supportive of the

[41] See Bundestagsdrucksache 11/5489, October 26, 1989; http://dip21.bundestag.de/dip21/btd/11/054/1105489.pdf (downloaded 2015-03-12)

Bundestag in its tasks as a legislative body, particularly when it came to shaping the conditions of scientific and technological change".[42]

Finally, on August 29, 1990, after long and intense debate on TA and its institutionalization, the German Bundestag signed the first contract with the Karlsruhe Nuclear Research Center for a three-year pilot phase. TAB was founded. Since then, it has been operated by the Institute for Technology Assessment and Systems Analysis (ITAS). After the conclusion of the pilot phase, the Bundestag decided on March 4, 1993, to establish a permanent advisory institution "Technology Assessment at the German Bundestag".[43][44]

The German TAB follows the organization model of "shared parliament-science involvement". Its work focuses solely on the German Bundestag. During the 25 years of its existence, the number of committees initiating and debating TAB studies has grown (see e.g. Ganzevles/van Est 2012:105). Although the federal and state ministries as well as research institutions, government agencies, companies, and interested members of the public follow the work of TAB with interest, the main addressee and only client is still the parliament. However, the demands of parliament or specifically of the members of the committee

---

42 See also "A brief history of the Office of Technology Assessment at the German Bundestag (TAB)" available on the TAB webpage http://www.tab-beim-bundestag.de/en/about-tab/history.html).

43 See Bundestagsdrucksache 12/4193, January 22, 1993; http://dip21.bundestag.de/dip21/btd/12/041/1204193.pdf (download 2015-03-12)

44 For the two following five-years-periods (until August 2003), the (then) Karlsruhe Research Center was commissioned to operate TAB on its own, and from September 2003 till August 2013 it cooperated in accordance with a decision of the Committee for Research, Technology and Technology Assessment with the Fraunhofer Institute for Systems and Innovation Research (ISI), Karlsruhe. On February 27, 2013, the Committee decided after a call for applications to commission the Karlsruhe Institute of Technology (KIT) to again run TAB for another five-year period (running until August 31, 2018), on which it cooperates in specific areas with the Helmholtz Center for Environmental Research (UFZ), the Institute for Future Studies and Technology Assessment (IZT), and the VDI/VDE Innovation + Technik GmbH.

on Education, Research, and Technology Assessment have also changed. Every five years ITAS applies for confirmation to operate TAB (together with consortium partners).

This recurring application process allows for the reconsideration of formats and methods. For example, over the years TAB has started to open to the public. From 2002 on, TAB and the committee have chosen several projects for organization of a public presentation of and debate on TAB reports to parliament with invited representatives from the media, research, industry, and civil society (see Ganzevles/van Est 2011:106). The necessity to involve the public in political decision-making processes is reflected from most existing TA institutions, – not merely in Germany.

What Steps to Take in the Future? Challenges and Ways Forward for Parliamentary TA in Changing Societies

Although the heterogeneity of the established parliamentary TA institutions has often been described, it is still worth focusing on the changes within this apparently established structure. "The concept as well as the organization of TA took remarkably different forms in different countries" (Vig 2000:367), and therefore the associated changes differ too. But regardless of the model of institutionalization, the societal challenges to TA must respond are similar: citizens affected by new technologies are increasingly being asked and willing to be directly involved in processes of political decision making; stakeholders with their specific knowledge in specific fields of technology are becoming increasingly important for the responsible use of technology; and politicians seek to decide on a well advised basis. And "[...] this involves the outputs of TA being expressed not as single, ostensibly definitive, results, but as plural and conditional reflections on whatever constitutes the most salient axes of sensitivity that emerge in the analysis" (Ely et al. 2015:61).

One way to open up TA is currently being practiced in the German TAB. The experience gathered in the regions concerned with planned electricity lines showed that measures are needed to enable a constructive dialogue to be conducted between local elected political representatives and citizens. Against the background that infrastructure projects decided at the German federal level have to be implemented at the local level, and that this kind of implementation is conflictual if it is just arranged top down, a TAB project should create a "solid basis in order that public discussion and participation procedures can be performed on an equal footing and – hopefully – with results that can be supported by all relevant stakeholders".[45] Involving the public has to be seen as a challenge, especially if it becomes part of the parliamentary process of consultation. Most of the European national parliaments strive for a long time to involve the public better and to increase the transparency of their work. And if it is true that the parliament as a whole and the parliamentary opposition in particular have the ability to contact citizens, groups, and other state institutions, in particular the government and the ministerial bureaucracy, then it is worthwhile for us to focus explicitly on the use of this communicative value (see also Herzog 1993:28).

Considering that TA analyses have to meet scientific standards and should provide recommendations for policy decision making, which implies an inherent need to include nonscientific knowledge as well, a specific challenge is visible. Apart from this, TA needs to be flexible with regard to sudden problems and current frictions within the sociotechnical system

45 Further information about the project "Balance of interests in infrastructure projects: Options for action with regard to local communication and organization" can be found on the web page http://www.tab-beim-bundestag.de/en/research/u10500.html (2015-3-16)

(e.g., accidents, environmental disasters). But in addition, TA attempts to function as a stable concept that provides knowledge for decision making based on the long-term perspective of influencing societal systems. Therefore, reflection on the particular disciplinary level with regard to these social systems also needs to be fulfilled. Having this in mind, it becomes clear that "pure" formalization of TA cannot end the debate about TA, its functions, and its development.

Another challenge to be mentioned is one of the results of the PACITA project which compared the political and societal conditions in countries which already have established parliamentary TA with those countries which do not. One of the findings was that TA almost always had a chance in countries where strong R&D infrastructures formed the basis of quite well developed economies and public welfare. But as the economic pressures increase even in these countries with established TA-infrastructures and as globalization strengthens the necessity to find appropriate responses to the challenges of our time, even in these countries TA is being asked to provide support for identifying "[...] socially sound and robust country specific innovation pathways ('constructive TA') and contribute to lower costs of trial and error learning" (Hennen/Nierling 2013:20). A joint European (or even international) TA network could function as an umbrella for both the established and the emerging TA institutions and national activities. Ideally, such a network will stabilize emerging TA activities by giving the national efforts an international frame, and the established TA institutions would be challenged to react to new demands by also learning from the new ones.

In order to strengthen a common identity, TA activities and the TA community should become international. Prototype activities such as joint projects with partners from several countries could be a productive starting point toward internationalization. "Joint work on TA-projects seems to be especially promising in this respect as it allows not only for the development of a shared problem orientation and an exchange and reflection on methodological approaches, but also for a cross-national analysis of specific questions in the field of science and technology" (Hennen/Nierling 2013:21). And international conferences offer a specific type of interaction and exchange within the heterogeneous TA community, too.

At the Berlin PACITA conference[46] in February, 2015, for example, not only scientists, but also stakeholders and politicians were invited to speak. The community realizes more and more that such formats help prepare one for embarking on complex challenges. The main aim of the conference was to offer contemporary formats of mutual learning and professional mobilization and combine TA-relevant activities such as risk communication, foresight, and policy analysis. "Especially, in the light of today's pressing challenges, it seems essential to provide spaces for 'discourse' of TA. Being a problem-oriented approach, TA needs areas of exchange and 'identity-shaping' particularly where its institutionalization is still unclear." (Scherz/Hahn 2015:19)

Our paper has examined the lessons that can be learned from the established TA institutions. While discussing what "established" means, one becomes aware that the established parliamentary TA institutions in Europe must stay vivid to reflect societal challenges and retain the ability to react institutionally.

---

46 http://berlinconference.pacitaproject.eu/

References

Bimber, B. (1996): The Politics of Expertise in Congress: The Rise and Fall of the Office of Technology Assessment. Albany, NY

Blair, P.D. (2013): Congress's Own Think Tank. Learning from the Legacy of the Office of Technology Assessment (1972-1995), New York

Deutscher Bundestag (1989): Zur Notwendigkeit und Ausgestaltung einer ständigen Beratungskapazität für Technikfolgen-Abschätzung und -Bewertung beim Deutschen Bundestag. *Drucksache* 11/4606, 30.5.89; http://dip21.bundestag.de/dip21/btd/11/046/1104606.pdf (downloaded 2015-05.21)

Ely, A., van Zwanenberg, P., Stirling, A. (2015): Experiments in Technology Assessment for International Development: What Are the Lessons for Institutionalisation? In: *Technikfolgenabschätzung – Theorie und Praxis (TATuP),* 1(2015), pp. 59-67; https://www.tatup-journal.de/downloads/2015/tatup151_elua15a.pdf (downloaded 2015-05-21)

Ganzevles, J., van Est, R. (2012): TA Practices in Europe. Deliverable 2.2 in the collaborative project on mobilization and mutual learning actions in European Parliamentary Technology Assessment; http://www.pacitaproject.eu/wp-content/uploads/2013/01/TA-Practices-in-Europe-final.pdf%20 (downloaded 2015-03-12)

Guston, D. (2001): Science and Technology Advice for Congress: Insights from the OTA Experience. Paper prepared for the workshop *Creating Institutional Arrangements to Provide Science and Technology Advice to Congress*, held in Washington, DC on 14 June 2001. http://ota.fas.org/legislation/st_advice_6-01.pdf (downloaded 2015-03-18)

Guston, D. (2003): Insights from the Office of Technology Assessment and Other Assessment Experiences. In: Morgan, M.G.; Peha, J.M. (eds.): *Science and Technology Advice for Congress*. Washington, DC, pp. 77-89

Hennen, L., Nierling, L. (2013): Expanding the TA Landscape. Deliverable 4.3 in the collaborative project on mobilization and mutual learning actions in European Parliamentary Technology Assessment; http://www.pacitaproject.eu/wp-content/uploads/2014/02/4.3_Expanding-the-TA-landscape.pdf (downloaded 2015-03-05)

Herzog, D. (1993): Der Funktionswandel des Parlaments in der sozialstaatlichen Demokratie. In: Herzog, D., Rebenstorf, H., Weßels, B. (eds.): *Parlament und Gesellschaft. Eine Funktionsanalyse der repräsentativen Demokratie*. Opladen, pp. 13-52

Keiper, A. (2004): Science and Congress. In: The New Atlantis 7, pp. 19-50

Petermann, Th., Scherz, C. (2005): Parlamentarische TA Einrichtungen in Europa als reflexive Institutionen. In: Petermann, Th.; Grunwald, A (eds.): *Technikfolgen-Abschätzung für den Deutschen Bundestag. Das TAB – Erfahrungen und Perspektiven wissenschaftlicher Politikberatung*. Berlin, pp. 271-294

Sadowski, J. (2015): Office of Technology Assessment: History, implementation, and participatory critique. *Technology in Society*, 42, pp. 9-20.

Sadowski, J., Guston, D. (2015): Technology Assessment in the USA: Distributed Institutional Governance. In: *Technikfolgenabschätzung – Theorie und Praxis (TATuP)*, 1(2015), pp. 53-59; http://www.tatup-journal.de/downloads/2015/tatup151_sagu15a.pdf (downloaded 2015-05-21)

Scherz, C., Hahn, J. (2015): TA conferences. Platforms for the Future. In: *VolTA Magazine, Science, Technology and Society in Europe*, No. 8, April 2015, p. 19; http://volta.pacitaproject.eu/wp-content/uploads/2015/03/VOLTA-num8_def_web.pdf (downloaded 2015-03-30)

Vig, N.J. (2000): Conclusions. The European Parliamentary Technology Assessment experience. In: Vig, N.J., Paschen, H. (eds.): *Parliaments and Technology. The Development of Technology Assessment in Europe*. New York, pp. 365-384

Vig, N.J., Paschen, H. (eds.) (2000): Parliaments and Technology. The Development of Technology Assessment in Europe. New York

Technology Assessment in Non-PTA Countries: An Overview of Recent Developments in Europe

Nuno Boavida and Antonio B. Moniz

Introduction

Despite recent activities to promote parliamentary technology assessment (PTA), there has not been a concrete increase in the number of these institutions in the West. PTA can be understood as an effort to mediate between science and politics and their knowledge claims (Ganzevles, van Est, and Nentwich 2014). In fact, PTA acts as an agent that mediates between two different processes (i.e., policy and science) when they can interact. This work aims to describe the latest developments in European countries or regions that lack a structure to develop PTA activities (named non-PTA). They are countries or regions where parliamentary-oriented TA activities have not yet resulted in a formal structure, but where TA-related activities can be detected to some extent. This chapter will concentrate on activities in Portugal, Wallonia, and other Central and Eastern countries such as the Czech Republic, Hungary, Poland, Lithuania and Bulgaria. Catalonia is mentioned as a specific case where a formal PTA structure exists but the way it is organized and financed is similar to the national and regional experiences at the non-PTA countries.

The focus on European non-PTA countries can provide clues for observing other developments in other parts of the world by emphasizing local developments. In fact, although the history of TA in Europe shows that it is possible to identify overall trends toward the establishment of TA, their local contexts might be more decisive for understanding the possible emergence of structures related to TA (Ganzevles, van Est, and Nentwich 2014).

Recently, a new collection of texts was published[47] concerning the historical paths of TA and the new efforts to institutionalize it in several countries around the world. The texts mostly addressed the different forms of TA that have developed and are developing Europe, in an effort to explain the external and internal contexts that might allow the launch of TA in some countries and regions. Most of this research was an outcome of the PACITA project whose aim was to stimulate reflection in regions and countries with established PTA organizations as well as in other European states with an interest in PTA. This paper is significantly based on these research outputs.

These issues can be of interest to those in the TA-related community and policy makers in Japan (and other East Asian regions) who do not have a formalized PTA system. The discussions and attempts being made in some European countries can give some indication of the challenges and possibilities for the institutional formalization of TA.

This paper argues that there are some elements of proximity in PTA between European countries and Japan. For example, Ganzevles, van Est and Nentwich (2014) write that a "number of scholars have looked for relationships among the arrival of different concepts for (parliamentary) TA in various countries and regions". The authors also mention that Meyer (1999) argues that PTA has broadened from an expert-based,

---

[47] The texts were published in English in the journal *Technikfolgenabschätzung – Theorie und Praxis* (2015, 24, 1).

parliament-oriented concept in the USA to concepts in Europe that have opened up to industry, other stakeholders, and the public at large.

Other authors such as Delvenne, Fallon, and Brunet (2011) suggest that PTA is evolving on an "overall reflexivity pathway", "on which some PTAs have moved farther than others". Furthermore, Ganzevles, van Est and Nentwich assert that "in this pathway, PTA has moved away from a mainly analytical activity that is 'aimed at providing decision-makers with an objective analysis of the effects of technology on political agenda, decision-making processes and society as a whole', and has opened up more to plurality and uncertainty, thereby 'acknowledging and responding to the limitations of modern traditions'" (Ganzevles, van Est and Nentwich, 2014: 298).

In the same way, the academic and political debate in Japan on the technology assessment options reveals similar elements about how to improve PTA activities. For example, Shiroyama et al. (2009: 5) points out that one of the problems of TA activities in Japan is its limited effectiveness with narrowly conceived feedback channels. The authors point to the need to pursue broader ways of communicating the TA results, such as identifying issues and setting the agenda (Shiroyama et al., 2009: 5).It therefore seems that the proximity between these countries is greater than the differences that separate them. In the following pages we will try to demonstrate this issue by considering some of the elements of European reality and experience.

Regional Processes of Institutionalization: The Cases of Catalonia and Wallonia

There are important European developments at the regional level. In fact, there is a success story in the Catalonia autonomous community of Spain, which has developed different formats for more than a decade. In 1999, the Catalan government created CACIT, an Advisory Commission on Science and Technology; in 2003, the Parliament urged the government to formally link CACIT to the Catalan Parliament; in 2008, CAPCIT[48] was formally established and started to function closer to a shared parliament-science model; and in 2009, CAPCIT became member of EPTA[49] (Böhle and Moniz 2015). Presently, CAPCIT can be seen as a "forum" composed of 10 parliamentarians and 10 representatives of the main scientific institutions of the region, producing reports and advice with no staff or budget (Böhle and Moniz 2015).

There has been another significant development in the TA landscape at the regional level. In fact, there is an emerging case of institutionalization of TA in the Wallonia region of the Belgium federation. The context is related to the development of STI policies in the region over the last fifteen years, which have become a basis of Walloon regional policy making, according to Delvenne et al. (2015). These developments were accompanied by an increase of interest in TA in regional governing bodies and with policy makers. Furthermore, TA activities gained momentum in Wallonia from the interaction between the University of Liège and regional representatives. These efforts led to a proposal for a parliamentary decree to create a TA institute linked to the parliament (Delvenne et al. 2015).

---

48 CAPCIT is the acronym for the Advisory Board of the Parliament of Catalonia for Science and Technology.

49 According to Böhle and Moniz (2015), CAPCIT is a mixed body composed by 20 members, half of them representing MPs and the other half the main scientific and technical institutions of Catalonia. "All the political parties are represented in this group, to which two members of the Presiding Board and the President of the Parliament – who is also the president of this mixed body – belong" (Böhle and Moniz 2015, 30).

A few years later, in May, 2011, two regional ministers announced a joint initiative to create a Walloon Institute of Technology Assessment. It emphasized the institute's role in policy making and in stimulating societal debate, its independence and location within the regional parliament, and its reliance on a network of experts and participatory methods, according to the authors. However, the creation of the institute was blocked by different conceptions of the Wallonia future: the TA institute should either work exclusively for the Walloon region (parliament and government) or also include the French community (e.g., the Brussels Capital Region) (see Delvenne et al. 2015).

At present, an approved parliamentary decree to solve the blockage "remains in the limbo of the legislative process" (Delvenne et al., 2015: 22). Also Hennen and Nierling (2014), referring to the TA activities in Wallonia, note this region already has a history of debate in its political system. Based on the study of Delvenne et al. (2012), they emphasize that there have been several initiatives in this region to set up TA capacities related to the government and the parliament. Just at the very moment when the research activities started, the decision to set up a TA institute was taken officially. Parliament and government are mentioned as the main addressees, but there is a lively political debate on the polity a TA institute should address: the Walloon region or the Wallonia–Brussels Federation.

The Portuguese Social Dynamic

The first initiatives to install a body providing scientific advice for science policy in Portugal date back to the 1960s, still during the dictatorship. In the early part of the decade, a special office was established to carry out assessment studies and economic studies to support the yearly national budget and the four year planning, named GEBEI

(Portuguese Office for Basic Studies on Industrial Economy, at the Ministry of Finance and Planning). In the end of the decade, the National Board of Scientific and Technological Research (JNICT) is created. Its mission was to plan, coordinate, and stimulate S&T research and to advise the government on national science policy.

Later, in the late 1980s, JNICT assumed the tasks of developing the national S&T system, sponsored the large national laboratories, and created a larger scientific community and new research centers (Böhle and Moniz 2015). JNICT managed a national program to support economically productive structures (co-financed by the structural funds from the European Community) and was responsible for research and publication of many studies on sectors, regions, and cases (Böhle and Moniz 2015). In the late 1980s, TA-like activities were mainly being carried out by the public sector (Gonçalves and João Caraça 1987).

TA-related activities continued to exist in different forms during the 1990s, when Portuguese experts and social scientists were involved in different European initiatives (Böhle and Moniz 2015). Furthermore, in the later part of this decade, TA activities were significantly influenced by the debate about the location of facilities to co-incinerate dangerous substances. During discussions about the danger posed to populations, the visible differences between scientists created a public perception of uncertainty and controversy (Alves 2011).

The debates were polarized and significantly adversarial, involving the affected populations, parliamentarians, members of government, and scientists. Overall, the debate led to an unprecedented shift in the role played by scientific commissions: their role moved from providing advice to exercising real decision-making power, in some matters leaving scientists to make decisions about political action, according to the authors. Since then, there has been a growing effort to ensure the independence of scientific committees and their members (Alves 2011). The dispute about co-incineration was long and marked by the "Not In My Back Yard" syndrome (Alves 2011). In fact, in 2014 the decision was still being questioned by a local group in the Constitutional Court.[50]

In addition, there were other important cases of public unrest with science, such as the threat of a H1N1 pandemic, the location of a third bridge across the Tagus River outfall, the location of the new airport in the Lisbon area, the plans for the high-speed railway, and recently a national legionella outbreak. These cases led to different solutions and sometimes involved loud public controversies between actors and stakeholders. Overall, the different solutions that were implemented contributed to an increase in the public's perception that scientific uncertainties and controversies relevant to policy making should be mediated by neutral actors.

The future developments in the national panorama of TA are still uncertain. On one hand, there are important national limitations to further TA developments. In fact, analysts mentioned the adverse impact of the insufficient involvement of stakeholders in decisions, the lack of a sound public opinion, the disconnect between the S&T system from economic structures, and the limited interactions between relevant ministries (Böhle and Moniz 2015). On the other hand, the combination of four interlinked dynamics provides room for more optimism. First, there are several PhD projects under development and preparing practitioners to deal with TA issues. In fact, the launching of a PhD program on TA at the University Nova Lisbon in 2009/10 created space to develop 20 research projects around TA issues in the country and generated a significant social dynamic around the topic. The research programs

50 "Co-Incineração de Resíduos Em Souselas No Tribunal Constitucional." *Lusa*. 17/01/2014.

cover topics from health TA studies, mobility and transport, brain-computer interfaces, innovation and STS, and cloud computing (Böhle and Moniz 2015).

Second, a national TA network named GrEAT exists since 2010 disseminating information and promoting regular contacts with other STS experts in Portugal. The network has been strengthened not only by an internal dynamic supported in the PhD program, but also by its involvement in parliament since 2010 and by its acceptance as an EPTA[51] observer institution in 2013.

Third, there is a consistent dynamic in the national parliament, rooted in the Commission for Education, Science and Culture. In 2009, parliament recognized the need to develop activities towards the development of PTA.[52] A report in 2013 suggested a proposal that failed to implement a TA unit inside the parliament.[53] The reasons for this failure are still unclear. Böhle and Moniz (2015) suggested that the failure rested on the lack of financial resources or in the organizational maladjustment of this unit, but a lack of consensus about the proposal is also conceivable. Nevertheless, recognition of the need for PTA led in 2014 to a series of hearings about the possible formats of the TA unit and PTA functions in parliament.[54], [55] At the present, several proposals are under discussion in parliament and GrEAT is contributing to overcoming the blockage

---

51 EPTA is the acronym of the network for *European Parliamentary Technology Assessment.*

52 Resolução da Assembleia da República No. 60/2009 – Aprofundamento das Actividades da Assembleia da República nas Áreas da Ciência e Tecnologia. Lisboa: Assembleia da República.

53 "Relatório Final – Avaliação Tecnológica Parlamentar." Comissão de Educação, Ciência e Cultura. 2013. Lisboa: Assembleia da República. http://avaliacaotecnologia.files.wordpress.com/2013/03/relatorio-rui-santos.pdf.

54 "Ata Número 178/XII/3a SL 19 Fevereiro 2014 – 10h00." Comissão de Educação, Ciência e Cultura. Lisboa: Assembleia da República.

55 "Ata Número 182/XII/3a SL 11 Março 2014 – 15h00." Comissão de Educação, Ciência e Cultura. Lisboa: Assembleia da República.

created in 2013 (Böhle and Moniz 2015). Fourth, there is a favorable external context where academic cooperation (particularly with ITAS/KIT[56]), European projects, and the EPTA network play a major role. The cooperation with ITAS/KIT has anchored strong scientific capabilities to the PhD program. For example, the support from ITAS/KIT allowed not just the development of several PhD theses, but also recent visits to Japan that helped to cement relations, exchange ideas, and launch this present book, among other activities.

The European projects have provided a framework to establish important international scientific and policy contacts. Lastly, the EPTA network allowed the recognition of GrEAT as a player in the national and international TA panorama, recognizing the network as a valid player in PTA debates in Europe. In sum, the context in Portugal combines adverse conditions with a significant social dynamic aiming to promote more TA activities in the country. Stronger TA activities are expected in the near future, as more PhD theses are discussed and these professionals play a role in the labor market.

Other Eastern and Central European Countries

TA is widely unknown in some Central and Eastern European countries. A possible explanation for this ignorance can be linked to the public's perception of science. In fact, science in Eastern countries served for a long time as an instrument of political propaganda, where scientists were ordered to create evidence to support the Soviet political regime (Leichteris 2015). Thus, it is not surprising that science-based policy

[56] ITAS/KIT is the acronym of the Institute for Technology Assessment and System Analysis at the Karlsruhe Institute of Technology.

advice is an area regarded with suspicion by the general public in these countries, according to Leichteris.

Furthermore, other problems for TA activity are related to a lack of understanding of the concept, the inflexibility of the current system, the danger of a politicization of such attempts, the concentration of decisions in the government rather than in the parliaments, and the lack of financing and skills (Leichteris 2015). However, there are some positive trends in these countries. In fact, the Czech Republic, Hungary, and Poland have had some experience in activities similar to TA, especially in technology foresight (Michalek et al. 2014; Leichteris 2015). The Czech Republic also revealed signals in health TA practice, which is starting to appear in Czech universities (Michalek et al. 2014).

Lithuania and Bulgaria were described as in transition towards problem-oriented research and interdisciplinary research (Leichteris 2015). Their TA-like activities often rely on consultancy work done by private companies, and is usually initiated by measures of the European Union or the OECD, according to Leichteris.

As mentioned by Hennen and Nierling (2014), it is apparent that all these advisory institutions (like science academies, research councils) "give strategic advice with regard to the future development of research and innovation strategies, which is motivated by national efforts to improve the competitiveness of the national economy ("economy first"). These authors also say that in Central and Eastern European countries this may be related to a great extent to the conflicting character of the ongoing and long-lasting political transition period from a nondemocratic system to a democratic one, using as a reference the work of Roland on transition processes (2002). Therefore, the overall situation of the Central and Eastern European countries towards TA can be described as unenthusiastic, although there are some TA-like activities being developed in some countries.

Conclusions

There are different levels of TA efforts in European countries and regions without PTA. Those with more PTA-like activities are Catalonia, Wallonia, and Portugal. There are also other dynamics with closer links to the parliament in Bulgaria and the Czech Republic, and other developments grounded in research and innovation structures in Hungary and Lithuania. Consequently, the possibilities for the emergence of TA in these countries and regions vary significantly. The example of Catalonian PTA started in 1999 and it was established in 2008 under the explicit will of the regional government and parliament. It now functions closer to a shared parliament-science model, producing reports and advice with no staff or budget. The Wallonia experience is also a significant dynamic in the European TA landscape and might even produce a TA institution in the short term. In the Portuguese case, unfavorable national characteristics challenge a dynamic academic base and the will of the national parliament, both significantly supported by a favorable international context. The experience of the Eastern and Central European countries are mostly marked by TA-like activities and face considerably adverse contexts. In sum, there are different levels of efforts in the European panorama, in which the local context appears to be relevant to understand what is going on under the present supportive European setting.

It seems to be true that different national contexts imply cultural settings and political specificities, which lead to different approaches to TA institutionalization. However, what appears to be more important, from our review of the cases, is to understand the extent of the social dynamic around the public production of knowledge and its links to the development of democratic institutions. In fact, these countries and regions have found their own and unique ways to solve their needs for TA by embedding the production of knowledge wherever possible in their own structures.

Jasanoff (2005) also mentioned the institutionalized practices by which members of a given society test and deploy knowledge claims used as a basis for making collective choices. In some cases, these social dynamics were linked to the local parliament and in others they remained far from it. But, most importantly, these dynamics do not necessarily need to be channeled through the institutionalization of a new specialized organization.

We can conclude that TA institutionalization in non-PTA countries appears to be dependent on the level of public production of knowledge. In fact, the presence or absence of S&T issues on the public agenda of these countries and regions affects the need for parliamentary policy advice: in their presence, S&T agenda pushes the need for TA advice by parliamentarians; in their absence, the promotion of innovation tries to keep up with globalization pressures and to generate economic growth, without significant demands for TA advice.

In the later case, the difficulties in deepening participation in democracy and the absence of transparent decision-making structures may lead to the lack of public involvement, trust, competence, and strategic long-term thinking. Nevertheless, it may happen that the public distrust in political systems and dissatisfaction with existing structures can be transformed into an opportunity or a barrier to institutionalization of independent policy advice. The answer to such a question may be answered by further studies on this issue.

References

Alves, Carlos Catalão. 2011. "Monitoring Policy and Research Activities on Science in Society in Europe (MASIS) National Report Portugal." Kongens Lyngby.

Böhle, Knud, and António Moniz. 2015. "No Countries for Old Technology Assessment? Sketching the Efforts and Opportunities to Establish Parliamentary TA in Spain and Portugal." *Technikfolgenabschätzung – Theorie Und Praxis* 24 (1): 29–44. doi:2199-9201. http://www.tatup-journal.de/tatup151_bomo15a.php.

Delvenne, Pierre, Nathan Charlier, Benedikt Rosskamp, and Michiel van Oudheusden. 2015. "De- and Re-Institutionalizing Technology Assessment in Contemporary Knowledge-Based Economies." *Technikfolgenabschätzung – Theorie Und Praxis* 24 (1): 20–28. doi:2199-9201. http://www.tatup-journal.de/tatup151_deua15a.php.

Ganzevles, Jurgen, Rinie van Est, and Michael Nentwich. 2014. "Embracing Variety: Introducing the Inclusive Modelling of (Parliamentary) Technology Assessment." *Journal of Responsible Innovation* 1 (3): 292–313. doi:10.1080/23299460.2014.968439. http://www.tandfonline.com/doi/abs/10.1080/23299460.2014.968439.

Gonçalves, Fernando, and João Caraça. 1987. "Towards Technology Assessment in Portugal." In *Technological Assessment – An Opportunity for Europe*.

Hennen, Leonhard and Nierling, Linda (2014). A next wave of Technology Assessment? Barriers and opportunities for establishing TA in seven European countries, *Science and Public Policy* (2014) pp. 1–15 [doi:10.1093/scipol/scu020]

Jasanoff, S. (2005) Designs on Nature. Science and Democracy in Europe and the United States. Princeton, NJ: Princeton University Press.

Leichteris, Edgaras. 2015. "Is There a Chance for TA? Reflections on the Perspectives for TA in Eastern/Central Europe." *Technikfolgenabschätzung – Theorie Und Praxis* 24 (1): 44–53. doi:2199-9201. http://www.tatup-journal.de/tatup151_leic15a.php.

Michalek, Tomáš, Lenka Hebáková, Leonhard Hennen, Constanze Scherz, Linda Nierling, and Julia Hahn. 2014. "Introduction." In *Technology Assessment and Policy Areas of Great Transitions*, 15–18. Prague. http://www.pacitaproject.eu/wp-content/uploads/2014/11/Conference-Book.pdf.

Roland, G. (2002) 'The political economy of transition', *Journal of Economic Perspectives*, 16: 29–50.

Shiroyama, H., G. Yoshizawa, M. Matsuo, and R. Hatanaka (2009). Activities without Institutionalization: Limits and Lessons of TA and TA-like Activities in Japan. *2009 Atlanta Conference Science and Innovation Policy*. Atlanta, IEEE,, http://dx.doi.org/10.1109/ACSIP.2009.5367849

Joint Fact Finding: Bridging the Evidence Gaps in Decision Making

Makiko Matsuo, Atsuo Kishimoto, Masashi Tachikawa, Masahiro Matsuura

Introduction

The Great East Japan Earthquake and the nuclear power plant accident in Fukushima of March 11, 2011, resulted in increased public distrust of decision makers and expert advisers. Part of the reason for this increased distrust is the confusion caused by the fact that (a) the decision makers did not sufficiently explain the basis of their decision making and (b) various experts expressed different opinions with regard to safety concerns. The objective of this paper is to introduce an "old but new" innovative approach, joint fact-finding (JFF), and explore its usefulness in the context of Japan, particularly after Fukushima. It considers what JFF can offer for decision making and its merits and challenges for institutionalization.

Background

Environment Surrounding Decision Making

The Fukushima event of March 11 highlights the characteristics of the environment surrounding today's decision making. The relationship – cause and effect – between science and society is becoming ever more complex, uncertain, and dynamic. The shorthand term "NaTech" describes an event like that of March 11, where the effects of technological risk were compounded by a natural disaster. Although the risks from the nuclear plant itself had of course been considered, the compounded impact of the risk of a Tsunami had not. The impact was beyond the scope of what had been envisioned: many factors interacted systematically, not only the health risks but also the environmental, economic, and societal factors. It is very hard to grasp the whole picture and nobody is sure of what the "right" decision(s) might be.

These characteristics of the world we live in – increasing complexity, uncertainty, and dynamism – mean that today's decision maker is in a very difficult position. These increasing characteristics require him/her to catch the "whole mapping of the factors" related to the object of his/her decision making and to consider thoroughly the tradeoffs between the factors and systematic or spillover effects. However, because of the limited time and resources and of public pressure, the politicians are prone to be obsessed with short-term interests and end up with myopic decisions that attract public populism, which in turn damages the regulator's credibility in the long run.

JFF: An Approach to Accountable Evidence

To avoid being bogged down in such a situation, it is indispensable for the decision maker to obtain evidence that is fully "accountable" (i.e., the evidence on which a particular decision is based should be transparent, sourced, and credited). This evidence is composed of various facts that form the basis for decision making. These facts involve both qualitative and quantitative facets and are not only limited to the facts provided/produced by the natural sciences but also include those produced by the social sciences.

JFF is an approach that helps one to obtain such inclusive evidence and to bridge the gaps in the evidence. JFF was originally proposed in the

US and there are many cases of its application to the environment. It is possible to see several examples, as in Ozawa and Susskind (1985), Ehrmann and Stinson (1999), McCreary et al (2001), Andrews (2002), Adler et al (2011), Karl et al (2007), or in Rofougan and Karl (2005). However, there seems to be no single common definition of JFF. In this paper, JFF is used to indicate a collaborative approach or process where JFF provides a forum for (a) co-framing the problem that needs to be addressed and (b) co-producing jointly found facts, including the areas of agreement and disagreement.

The underlying philosophy for seeing the "facts" is different from what we term the "old facts" view, where scientific "facts" are objective, neutral, and unbiased and therefore any disputes can be resolved by seeking the right facts. We consider that "facts" must be enlarged to include various facts, not only scientific ones, but also scientific assumptions and the framing behind the facts presented (and these may become very close to values) as well as other further facts about social, economic, and legal facts (see Figure 2 in Sect. 2.2). It acknowledges that scientific facts should be distinct from values but it also accepts that facts are often not totally free from values. Decision makers should grasp the whole picture of the facts surrounding the issue, which comes back to the concept of acountable evidence.

iJFF and JFF cases and the Development of Guidelines

JFF in Japan

In response to the increasing public distrust in science and policy decision making following Fukushima, there has been a growing interest in JFF in Japan. For example, the Ministry of Economy, Trade and Industry convened a series of symposia on the geological disposal of high-level radioactive wastes, and one of these symposia was held using the JFF approach (February, 2013). However, this is still a rare case of the utilization of the JFF approach by the ministries. JFF continues to be underappreciated by decision makers, and decision makers are still at the stage of exploring the usefulness of such an approach.

The iJFF (Integrating Joint Fact-Finding into Policy-Making Processes) project is one such effort. It is funded by the Research Institute of Science and Technology for Society (RISTEX) of the Japan Science and Technology Agency (JST), which is affiliated with the Ministry of Education, Culture, Sports, Science and Technology. It is a three-year project (2011–2014). The objectives of the project are to explore the applicability of JFF approaches in the Japanese context by conducting three action research projects (in the fields of food safety, energy policy, and marine spatial planning). It is also aimed at networking with similar fields of practice, such as the technology assessment and risk analysis communities. We disseminated the outcomes of our research to these communities to obtain feedback for consideration. The following sections provide some of the insights obtained from this iJFF project.

The JFF Case of Radionuclides in Food

The iJFF project conducted an experimental JFF dialogue on radionuclides in food. The spread of radionuclides as a result of the accident at Fukushima Dai-ichi nuclear power plant has contaminated food around Fukushima and the neighboring prefectures. The risk of radionuclides in food was one of the sources of public confusion after the earthquake. Since the low risk of radionuclides at low doses is inherently uncertain, experts and consumer groups expressed a variety of opinions in the media, books, and newspapers. There was a clear need for JFF among experts, in the first place to identify the source of their divergent views. The iJFF food safety group engaged in a "pre-JFF activity" to consider possible sources of disagreement among the experts (literature reviews and interviews etc.) and then held a JFF event at the 26th annual meeting of the Society for Risk Analysis in Japan (November 17, 2013). The JFF session brought together leading experts on risk assessment/management from the food safety community and the radiation community.

The following provides a brief summary of our findings in the food safety group's JFF activities (for more details, refer to Matsuo et al.'s (forthcoming) paper). First, many disciplines are actually interested in the risk posed by radionuclides since the radiation is used in variety of fields (Figure 1). In contrast to the traditional view that science speaks with one voice, each of these disciplines has developed its own way of thinking and had little interaction with the other disciplines. Moreover, until the Fukushima incident, the food safety community had never considered the risk posed by radionuclides seriously, and there was no expert on the risk posed by radionuclides in the food safety community. Although one should not overgeneralize, there are differences in the attitudes of scientists toward radiological risk depending on the discipline. Since there has been less interaction between and among the disciplines, there was no general consensus about the appropriate way to treat uncertainty.

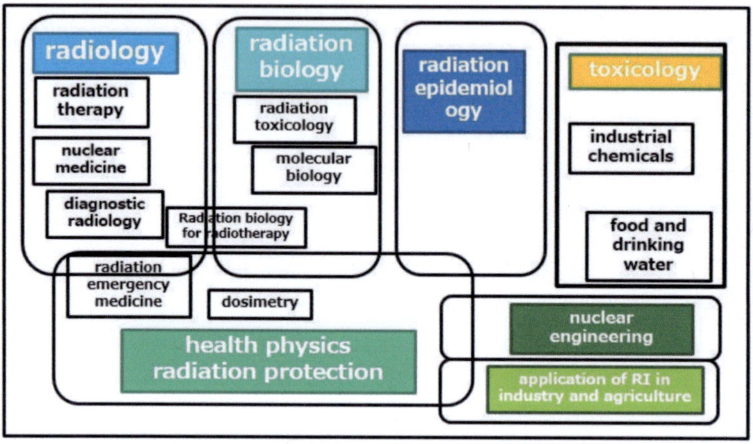

Figure 1: Many disciplines related to the risks posed by radionuclides

Furthermore, there were different approaches towards uncertainty. In fact, at least three ways of handling uncertainty in general terms were identified. The first approach treats uncertainty in risk assessment as equivalent to "virtually safe". This approach considers a risk scenario to be safe unless it is proven to be harmful since the scientific facts (i.e., the scientific data etc.) cannot identify the exact harm. The second approach is the exact opposite to the first approach. It considers uncertainty itself to be virtually harmful since you never know what would happen until proven safe. Taking this position, you would have to endeavor to achieve "zero risk".[57] The third approach is the risk-based approach. The biggest difference from the previous two is that this approach uses scientific assumptions (for example, the linear no threshold or LNT model) in the analysis. The existence of risk is acknowledged

57 The European Commission deals with this dichotomy by introducing the criteria that the precautionary action that you take should be proportionate to the harm you wish to avoid (European Commission, 2000).

and the focus is on the consideration of what is the virtually safe level or appropriate level of protection.

The unique dimension identified from the JFF exercise was the consideration of other facts besides scientific ones. As mentioned above, the risk posed by radionuclides is a very complex issue. It involves risk trade-off issues not limited to health risks but also including other socioeconomic risks. In addition, there was a difference in management approaches between food risk control and radiological protection in general. The methods of treating the acceptable level of risk were different.

To sum up, the JFF approach reveals the existence of different facts that constitute the evidence for decision making in managing the risk posed by radionuclides in food. The identified facts can largely be categorized into three boxes (See Figure 2); (a) the scientific facts based on conventional or traditional science, (b) the facts based on scientific assumptions, (c) the other facts such as economic, societal, ethical, or legal factors. It should be noted that in the selection of facts for evidence in the final decision making, interaction between the facts is needed.

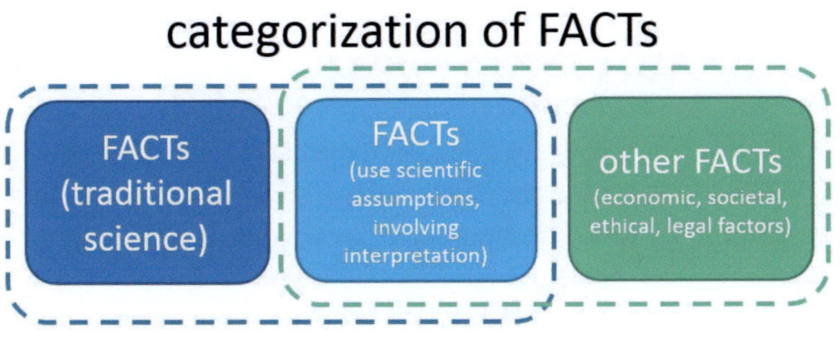

Figure 2: Categorization of facts

Development of a Set of Principles for JFF

In addition to the experimental JFF activities, the iJFF project developed a set of principles for conducting JFF exercises, taking into account the lessons learned from various experiments with JFF in Japan, a literature review, and discussion with a variety of experts at symposia. The principles are listed in Table 1.

Table 1: A set of principles for conducting JFF exercises

(1)	Evidence should be acquired by the parties.
(2)	A common understanding about what constitutes evidence should be explored.
(3)	Evidence should cover comprehensively the varieties of relevant disciplines.
(4)	Beware of the uncertainty (or unavailability) of evidence.
(5)	Be conscious about identifying who the parties are.

Conclusion: The Future of JFF

The Usefulness of JFF

Several lessons have been identified or reconfirmed by our experience in the iJFF program. Firstly, JFF has the potential to transform the decision-making processes, from top-down and linear to a more collaborative approach. We stress the "joint" and "fact" aspects of JFF. By "joint," the scope can be expanded through interaction, since this can bring together actors and their frameworks: not only expert and lay persons, experts and politicians, but also expert and expert (in the same or different disciplines) or experts and politicians and lay persons, for example.

It can change the knowledge flow from "expert as knowledge provider" to "expert and/or other actors as knowledge producers".

Secondly, the proposed categorization of facts resulting from the JFF food experiment is useful in making explicit the acknowledgement of the evidential basis. By explicitly acknowledging the different categories of facts, it encourages decision makers and stakeholders to avoid ignoring the implicit consideration of prioritization or trade-off decisions embedded in different categories of facts.

Lastly, the JFF approach challenges the view that science speaks with one voice. It questions the assumptions of science in policy making and provides an opportunity for reconsidering the conventional way of thinking, which can stimulate a learning process among those involved. All this contributes to promoting the opening up of evidence and thus can provide policy alternatives. By giving explicit reasons for the policy choice on the basis of the identified evidence, it can stimulate more transparent and evidence-based decision making. It enhances the quality, the credibility, and legitimacy of the decision to be taken and should contribute to building trust.

Challenges to an Institutionalization of the JFF Approach

JFF can be used stand-alone or can be embedded in any step of the policy cycle, from agenda setting to implementation and monitoring (Adler et al 2011). The proposed approach can be embedded in the existing institutional arrangements such as the risk analysis frameworks and technology assessment (TA). Since JFF examines various facts associated with complex science and technology issues, thus helping decision making, it can be considered a variant of TA.[58]

However, in Japan, JFF is yet to be institutionalized in formal policy-making processes. There are two main challenges to the institutionalization of JFF in Japan. One is that our proposed JFF is an approach and not a determined methodology. It is a kind of approach to the issue but does not prescribe detailed steps or criteria to be followed. The design for organizing a JFF event can (and should be) considered in the context of the desired objective. It allows flexibility but might be regarded as less straightforward or understandable for the practitioners.

The second challenge may be an obstacle stemming from the unwillingness on the part of decision makers who mistakenly believe this kind of effort to be "a threat to their authority," as was pointed by Susskind (2008). Decision makers might resist the idea of "opening up" the possible alternatives besides the one they opt for. However, it is important to keep in mind that opening up the discourse to facts can also contribute to closing down some policy options. JFF can make it possible to identify many facts. This inclusiveness helps decision makers to consider what should be prioritized and to narrow down the policy choices. It helps them to explain the reasons for the choices being made. This in turn will contribute to restoring confidence and trust.

---

58 However, there are some differences (in a relative sense) in terms of issue scope and time scope. In terms of issue scope, while JFF is more focused and issue or problem oriented, TA assesses the broader impacts of a specific technology. With regard to time scope, JFF puts more emphasis on the analysis of the current situation but TA looks at the "now to future" impact. JFF is similar to participatory TA and constructive TA but starts from the premise that expert advice itself is not "given."

Note

The main body of this paper is based on the Matsuo et al (forthcoming) Joint Fact-Finding (JFF) of the Risk posed by Radionuclides in Food.

Acknowledgement

Integrating Joint Fact-Finding into Policy-Making Processes (iJFF) is a project of the Research Institute of Science and Technology for Society (RISTEX) of the Japan Science and Technology Agency (JST) (November 2011 to November 2014).

References

Adler, P., Bryan, T., Mulica, M. and Shapiro, J.: Humble Inquiry: The Practice of Joint Fact Finding as a Strategy For Bringing Science, Policy and the Public Together, mediate.com, 2011.
[http://www.mediate.com/articles/AdlerJoint.cfm]

Andrews, C.J. (2002) Humble Analysis: The Practice of Joint Fact-Finding, Praeger.

Ehrmann, J. R. and Stinson, B. L. (1999) Joint Fact Finding and the use of technical experts, in Susskind, L., McKearnan, S., and Thomas-Larmer, J., eds., The Consensus Building Handbook: Thousand Oaks, Calif., Sage Publications, p. 377.

Graham, John D. and Wiener, Jonathan B. (1997) Risk vs. Risk: Tradeoffs in Protecting Health and the Environment, Harvard University Press.

McCreary, S.T.,Gamman, J.K., Brooks, B. (2001) Refining and Testing Joint Fact-Finding for Environmental Dispute Resolution: Ten Years of Success, Mediation Quarterly, Vol 18 (4).

Karl, H. A., Susskind, L. E., Wallace, K. H. (2007) A Dialogue, not a Diatribe, Issue of Environment. Vol. 49 (1), 20–34.

Ozawa, C. and Susskind, L.E. (1985) Mediating Science-Intensive Policy Disputes, Journal of Policy Analysis and Management, Vol. 5 (1), 23–39.

Renn O. (2008) Risk Governance: Coping with Uncertainty in a Complex World, EarthScan.

Renn, O., Klinke, A. and van Asselt, M. (2011) Coping with Complexity, Uncertainty and Ambiguity in Risk Governance: A Synthesis, in AMBIO – A Journal of the Human Environment, Vol. 40 (2), 231–246.

Rofougaran, N. L. and Karl, H. A. (2005) San Francisquito Creek – The Problem of Science in Environmental Disputes, in USGS Professional Paper 1710.

Matsuo M., Kishimoto A., Tachikawa M. (forthcoming), Joint Fact-Finding (JFF) of the Risk of Radionuclides in Food

Matsuo M. (2013), Retrospection and Prospection Concerning the Japanese food safety Governance from an Institutional Analysis, Journal of Risk Analysis Japan, vol,23, pp.127–135,

Matsuo M. (2013), Restructuring Japanese Food Safety Governance: Institutional Changes and Future Challenges, the European Food and Feed Law Review, Vol. 8 No.4

Susskind, L. (2008), Arguing, Bargaining, and Getting Agreement, The Oxford Handbook of Public Policy, Edited by Robert E. Goodin, Michael Moran, and Martin Rein

Part II

TA under Pressure: A Challenge of Interdisciplinarity/Transdisciplinarity

Global Pressure – Local Transition: The German "Energiewende" as an Interdisciplinary Research Problem in the Helmholtz Alliance ENERGY-TRANS

Christian Büscher[59]

Introduction

Global events have effects on local policies. Energy supply is a global event, where three major issues arise on local levels too. *First*, environmental degradation which severely affects the local population (e.g. oil spillage in coastal regions or on oil fields in Latin America, Africa, Russia etc.) and dangerous accidents (e.g. nuclear power plants in the USA, Ukraine, or Japan). *Second*, the combination of a global demand for energy sources which is increasing and an availability of energy carriers which is decreasing (e.g. "peak oil"). *Third*, changes in the climate system and the struggle for global political solutions. People are preoccupied with these issues and therefore various reactions occur at local levels: large technology projects are feared and opposed, values and lifestyles change and political programs are modified.

The German public has long debated the advantages and disadvantages of nuclear technology and fossil energy generation, eventually leading to

59 KIT-ITAS, Helmholtz Alliance ENERGY-TRANS

the project – some call it experiment – of the German Energy System Transition (Energiewende).

The German Energy System Transformation (hereafter the "GEST") is a political program to exploit renewable energy sources (RES), by developing and implementing technical systems. It is increasingly apparent that this energy system transformation poses socio-technical problems which require more than merely technical solutions. These socio-technical problems require, moreover, social solutions; both on the level of the energy system as a functional unit (of organizations, regimes and networks), as well as on the level of individual action. The common theme underlying these socio-technical problems is the balance of *stability* and *change*. On one hand, new technical and organizational paradigms are necessary; on the other hand, everybody expects reliability, security and affordability of energy provision.

Tensions and breaches arise on distinctive levels of the energy system:

- On the functional level, the continued paradigm holds that energy is produced by large technical systems; however, this paradigm is strained by the new, competing idea of energy production by decentralized units.
- On the organizational level of regimes and networks, the dominance of large enterprises obstructs the inclusion of manifold small-sized actors operating in niches.
- On the level of households and individual action, the unreflecting attitude that energy is always available (energy flat rate) is still widespread, although it must be replaced by a more active role of 'prosumers' who not only consume electricity, but also produce it.

The energy system is understood, by the Helmholtz Alliance ENERGY-TRANS, "as a complex socio-technical system." Based on this perspective, the Alliance "conducts interdisciplinary research into the systemic interactions of the envisioned energy transition." It reunites over sixty "social and political scientists, psychologists and philosophers, economists, legal scholars, engineers and systems analysts", who conduct interdisciplinary research "on the interplay between technical potentials, innovation processes, user behavior, political and economic conditions (…), conflicts and management processes."[60] This paper addresses sociological research problems along the common referential research theme of *stability* and *change*.

Premises of the *Energiewende*

From its beginnings in the 1970s, Technology Assessment has sought to comprehensively assess the social, economic, political, legal, technical and ecological consequences of purposeful, planned action. The GEST is a program where political action tries to determine the course of the overall development of a crucial infrastructure system. We neither know what the consequences of this endeavour will be, nor how far-reaching they will be. However, it seems reasonable that technology assessment can only understand the consequences of an extensive political program, if it exposes, analyzes, and assesses the latent premises. These premises have to be met, in order to yield a successful transformation – as widely envisioned. It is important to debate the answers to questions such as:

- Are the assumed premises realistic?
- Who will be affected by the consequences?
- Are there any alternatives which are not discussed enough?

---

60 See the introduction to the project: www.energy-trans.de/english/21.php, 19.5.2015

Scenarios of possible developments are derived from scientific visions, expectation statements and policy papers about the GEST. This plethora of statements from scientists, engineers, economists, politicians and other stakeholders needs to be analyzed in a multi-dimensional fashion, emphasizing distinctive problems beyond the usual economic cost-benefit rationale.

The GEST is based upon the following three premises which pose particular research challenges from a sociological perspective.

First Premise: System Change despite Stability

The GEST implies substantive changes in enduring technological paradigms regarding the organization of energy supply (generation, transportation, distribution and consumption). Moreover, the transformation requires a change in market coordination, because the process of liberalization enforces an unbundled energy economy with new laws, regulations, taxes, and subsidiaries to stimulate, limit, and control all transactions. However, the transformation is expected to proceed with a maximum stability of energy provision.

Therefore, recent research on the energy system transition tries to explain the relationship between *stability* and *change* of socio-technical systems and regimes: Whilst stability provides orientation and allows for action, change makes learning, innovating and intelligent adaptation to new circumstances possible (most prominent: Geels 2004). Hence policy makers and actors need to decrease resilience in some parts of the energy system, while increasing it in others (Strunz 2014) to unlearn, i.e. to "exnovate", common practices and knowledge (Gross and Mautz 2015), or to substitute dominant "field logics" (Fuenfschilling and Truffer 2014), or to destabilize regimes (Geels 2014). The appropriate balance of stability and change is particularly important in the context of critical infrastructures, where large scale failures may have catastrophic consequences.

Despite the need for change, stable orientations – like rules, norms, and routines – are necessary to absorb uncertainty in a complex environment. Therefore, these orientations should not be shattered all at once, or too abruptly. From a global, systemic perspective, the normative goal of sustainability has to be accompanied by measures to ensure the sustainment of current operation. Organizational theory frames this problem as the balance between "redundancy" and "variation" (Luhmann 1988b): Both are indispensable, but too much variety causes volatile, erratic behavior, whilst too much redundancy causes inertia, lock-ins and path dependencies.

Second Premise: System Transition as a Project

The political program of the GEST is usually depicted as a project with an identifiable starting point which begins the planned process and results in the desired end-results: affordable and reliable, but more sustainable, energy. The whole endeavor has been initiated based upon the assumption that the end-state will be superior to the current state. However, nobody knows whether these far-reaching and broad goals will be reached, since they depend on projections about possible, and therefore contingent, futures.

In order to launch the GEST, a large portion of uncertainty has to be overcome, the knowledge about non-knowledge has to be ignored, and the possibility of failure has to be erased from contemplation. In order to increase our motivation to act, we rely on shared *ideologies* to reduce alternatives and fade out the corresponding consequences to a minimum

(Brunsson 2007:46). The idea of the *Energiewende* might be such a highly functional ideology, though it is also highly precious and fragile. Already, discussions about the absence of "*the* master-plan" are growing louder. The observation of an un-organized, chaotic transformation process erodes core assumptions of the *Energiewende* ideology.

Moreover, there will not be a final state of affairs in the sense of a consummated GEST, for, as a large technical system, it constitutes a linked series of socio-technical problems. This means that novel solutions at one end of the system (e.g. RES) will always produce new problems at the other end (e.g. long distance transportation and storage):

> *"At the largest scales, principles of increasing speed, volume, and efficiency drive the entire economy, with each increase in one area creating a reverse salient in another" (Edwards 2004:209).*

The inevitable obstacles, miscues and unwanted consequences will lead to disappointments on the way. More importantly, if these negative events gain symbolic value, they may endanger the whole project because – in their function as symbols – they undermine the idea(l) of the project, and therefore the program stands to lose the support of the public.

Third Premise: 'Prosumers' as Rational Actors

Visions of 'smart grids', 'demand-side management', 'virtual power plants', 'electric vehicle management' and 'energy prosumers' illustrate assumptions about the changing role of the general public: Former service abiders are to become active service providers (Depuru, Wang, and Devabhaktuni 2011; Ramchurn et al. 2012).

The promise of a new technology which makes energy provision easier can only be fulfilled with a sharpened distinction between a simple operating interface and a complex technology underlying this interface. Accordingly, 'prosumers' must forsake control for the benefit of *trust*. The general public cannot control the system, nor the consequences of their actions, and therefore have to rely on trust. From a functionalist point of view, the overall system can only realize its potential if prosumers possess *actionability*.

To participate in energy system services, the general public has to develop confidence in the technical, economic, and legal programs of this system. Without trust and confidence, the public cannot successfully exploit the chances and opportunities of future developments. Public distrust – or even a mere lack of public trust – could be reflected in passive, fatalistic attitudes, or lead to a search for autonomy, or obstructing action. Overconfidence, on the other hand, could lead to hazardous actions. As a consequence, trust, rather than public acceptance, may well constitute the *reverse salient* of energy system transformations.

Sociotechnical Problems

For the purpose of interdisciplinary research, strict theoretical definitions which all research branches have to align to are not helpful. In our experience, it is most helpful to reach an understanding about shared referential problems, to which different lines of research contribute with their respective theories and methods. For the GEST, it does not help to insist on a single definition of the system under observation, i.e. the elements, interrelations, boundaries, mechanisms of reproduction, input-output-relations, etc. Nonetheless, there is the need for cognitive integration to the degree that every statement resulting from the interdisciplinary research effort ought to refer to a common referential problem.

For the GEST, the various disciplines often refer to the concept of a 'socio-technical system', because the system's transformation depends both on social and on technical variables. This concept incurs various theoretical and methodological difficulties, for example in terms of exactly selecting the included from the excluded elements influencing the operation of such a system. Another difficulty lies in analyzing the relationship between the technical and the social components in more depth than just stating that they constitute a "seamless web" (Hughes 1986). The notion of a seamless web presupposes that heterogeneous elements are aligned to fulfill the system's overarching purpose (service), i.e. providing power, and that as single (sub-) units these elements fulfill a certain function within the system: power plants provide, transmission lines transmit, control-units measure, adjust and regulate, etc. Socio-technical systems comprise "linkages between elements necessary to fulfill societal functions" (Geels 2004:900) and

> *"socio-technical regimes themselves tend to be understood in terms of networks of actors and institutions clustered around the fulfillment of social and economic functions" (Smith, Stirling, and Berkhout 2005:1507).*

However, by referring to the reproduction of the system (i.e. maintaining operation), or the boundaries or the identity of such a system, we encounter the multi-purpose design of organizations involved in networks of service provision such as electricity, health, telecommunications, water management etc. This can be illustrated by private enterprises involved to some extent in public electricity provision while, at the same time, having to maintain business and compete on markets (i.e. in other contexts than electricity services) – no matter where revenue comes from, it has to be secured.

Consequently, it is not far-fetched to state that the reproduction of a social system, such as a private company, is primarily a self-serving purpose and thus not necessarily aligned to the overall purpose of an energy system – i.e. providing electricity. In this regard, the concept of a socio-technical system as a closed, seamless entity of heterogeneous elements cannot capture the fact that organizations contribute to the system in more ways than their planned operations. In fact, the constantly evolving system produces solutions for problems and problems for solutions simultaneously: "The overall [socio-technical] system can be fruitfully described as posing a linked series of socio-technical problems" (Edwards 2004:209). The introduction and implementation of RES during the last decades has replaced carbon dependent energy provision and that fact in itself creates new challenges for storage and transportation (for example for electricity), for the organization of production (market interaction, regulation), and for legislative decision-making regarding the installation of corresponding infrastructures (power plants, physical networks).

Rather than aligning research to common theoretical definitions about socio-technical systems, it seems helpful to expose shared socio-technical problems. In this sense, we refer to three analytically distinct dimensions of the energy system: *structure*, *institution* and *operation*, and extract three respective socio-technical problems.

Complexity of Future Energy Systems

Experts increasingly experience the energy system operation's complexity.[61] The new and evolving energy system comprises a greater number of heterogeneous technical and social elements and, therefore, new and still evolving relationships between those elements. Changes in the *technical* organization of production impose complex consequences, just as changes in the regulatory structure create complex effects on the *social* organization of production (see for a useful heuristic: Mayntz 2009).

With the widespread introduction and integration of RES the problem of 'volatility' becomes manifest. 'Volatility' describes the possibility of a range of fluctuating occurrences and leads to the problem of control. In other words, we are uncertain about subsequent events, because various futures are contingent, and thus are we exposed to undertaking risks. Within the electricity domain, volatility is a problem for operators who must sustain the equilibrium of electricity inflow and outflow within the physical network of transportation and distribution of electrical power.

Nowadays, instead of basing their calculations on a few nuclear and coal based power plants with a constant output, operators must calculate with a multitude of 'producers' who do not constantly feed into the network (e.g. because weather conditions determine the output). To not only achieve greater control over the emerging energy infrastructure, but also to increase the overall efficiency (by aligning generation to consumption and *vice versa*), far-reaching visions of smart technologies are brought to bear on the domain of the energy system. Many of these visions are inspired by progress in information and communication technologies and, more specifically, in electronic data processing.

---

[61] Result from our field research in 2012/2013 (results will be published in 2015).

Many proponents of 'smart technology' envision greater developments than the automation-paradigm such as artificial intelligence and, particularly, self-monitoring and self-healing functions. We can expect the existence of machines as "autonomous actors" under human supervision, but not necessarily under human control (Amin 2001; Ma et al. 2009; Ramchurn et al. 2012). Throughout the infrastructure system, we already face emergent behavior which cannot entirely be explained with reference to the behavior of the individual elements of the system (Kröger and Zio 2011:195). If autonomous, self-modifying and learning non-human actors will be implemented in future grid control programs, then the issue of control will be paramount. In addition, as the reader will discover below, questions about trust and the delegation of control will ensue.

Based on current visions, we have to expect the emergence of more intertwined technical networks, such as local systems connected to larger networks, which will themselves depend on other enabling structures (such as the transportation system).

"In general, infrastructures are not systems. Instead, they are networks or webs that enable locally controlled and maintained systems to interoperate more or less seamlessly" (Edwards et al. 2007:12).

Large technical systems evolve into ubiquitous and reliable structures, which operate on national and transnational scales to distribute widely shared resources. More importantly, the degree of control depends on whether the structure is:

- a local system which is centrally organized and controlled,
- a linked systems, i.e. a network, where control is distributed (partially or wholly) among the nodes of the networks, or
- a network of networks, i.e. a web, which is based primarily on coordination rather than control (Edwards et al. 2007:12).

Consequently, new forms of market transaction need to be coordinated and supervised. European legislature has introduced rules on "unbundling" which impose operational disintegration on the current energy system – a system which has grown according to the requirements of central control. Künneke (2008:239) claims that

"[from an] institutional perspective, the electricity value chain seems to evolve towards unbundling and specialization, whereas technology is based on integrated system planning".

Some researchers warn that unbundling may cause a loss of control and, consequently, a deterioration of the quality of service (Künneke 2008). To be more precise, 'unbundling' usually refers to the separation of functional subunits *within* the system. However, in the case of energy provision, 'liberalization' constitutes a political program that is *exogenous* to the energy system. It is the attempt to create and expand markets in highly functionally integrated domains, by forcing disintegration.

Accordingly, the question arises how changes in governance constellations can buffer this kind of misalignment. From a sociological point of view, it is crucial to deal with the functionalist problem of ignorance, non-transparency, complexity, decision-uncertainty and risk in the face of large socio-technical systems. The typical response from scientists and engineers involves promoting more technology to solve these problems. That is not false – but only half the truth. There are many indications that we experience a 'dialectic' development with the widespread use of electronic data processing: Firstly, more data processing capabilities, but also the need to develop methods of selecting useful data resulting in actual information. Secondly, more productivity, but also new frictions if conventional organizational structures are forced to incorporate new technologies. Thirdly, more transparency through elaborate models about organizational processes, but also more complicated algorithms which only specialists can understand – algorithms that are intertwined in even more complicated networks which no single person can control.

What is potentially a problem for scientific experts, is certainly a problem for lay persons. Many people are now more aware of the problems that a 'network society' entails – and these problems do not only concern the ongoing surveillance by state agencies and by private companies. People experience more convenience with the use of internet technology, but at the same time they also experience how dangerous it is, exposing them to fraud in internet banking, as well as other hazards during socializing, shopping and using 'smart homes'. People realize how helpless they are. These threats are becoming more and more sophisticated, leaving little possibility for most of us to actually comprehend what is going on technically, let alone how to protect ourselves.

Stable Expectations and Learning

Because of the pressure which global society faces today, proposals to transform local infrastructure systems are prevalent in a variety of policy programs. Researchers, too, also write about the necessity to change systems (Geels 2014:2). Nevertheless, the expectations about the output and service of socio-technical systems remain stable, since socio-technical systems are defined with regard to their purpose. Although it is yet unknown how exactly the system will evolve, it is widely expected that the future energy system will provide energy. The energy system is not only a (infra-)structure, but also an *institution:* the notion of an 'institution' indicates robust social orientation in the sense of generalized expectations, viable over long periods of time.

According to some authors, the strength of a regime depends on the degree of *institutionalization* of core elements which contribute to its stability and function. Transition research is looking for structural densifications of this kind (as regimes), and it tries to explain how these densifications change (Smith et al. 2005; Grin, Rotmans, and Schot 2010; Fuenfschilling and Truffer 2014). In this way, institutions are at the heart of transition research.

However, research on institutions also needs to focus on maintaining capacities for learning, experimenting and transition *within* socio-technical systems. In particular, the relationship between structure and institution is emphasized to uncover ways of directing transitions onto a more sustainable path (Weber and Rohracher 2012:1041). On one hand, the notion of 'structure' indicates the quality and the quantity of single system elements unified by a particular purpose in the factual dimension. *Institutions*, on the other hand, indicate *how* these elements relate to each other and unravel rules that follow. Hence we understand the term 'institution' to mean a complex of expectations attributed with certain values which are generally shared among various actors in specific domains.

Many German researchers consider the GEST to be a large socio-technical experiment that entails a high degree of uncertainty and non-knowledge, but is an unavoidable process, since there are no viable alternatives (Gross and Mautz 2015:144). From the perspective of structure and control theories, there is a need to adjust the degree of coupling (loose/ tight) of experimental projects to the existing systems. According to normal accident theory, tight coupling and non-linear interactions cause dangerous settings in socio-technical systems (Perrow 2011). Nonetheless, local energy experiments must be conducted in real life constellations, yet without compromising the entire system when (inevitable) errors occur. Only by trial and error, can experiments generate knowledge that serves as a foundation for crucial developments.

From the perspective of institution theories, the actors must un-learn conventional, successfully applied technologies, norms and habits. That is valid for all organizations and professionals in the field, but also for the general population. German citizens are still getting used to the liberalization of gas and electricity markets and learning (or not) how to compare prices and services to select an appropriate supplier. For example, representatives of a traditional communal energy supplier (Stadtwerke) in Germany, explain that they still have long-standing customers who pay their monthly bills personally at the counter – and in cash. That is why they still operate a cash counter. The other side of the behavioral spectrum shows customers who are very much accustomed to comparing prices, substituting suppliers, and changing contracts every year. A major difficulty of institutional theory is determining the successful balance between stable orientations regarding service provision and changes, in form of innovations, learning and un-learning.

Actionability Despite Non-transparency

Many researchers deem 'acceptance' the crucial variable of a successful transformation of an energy system:

> *"No problem is more stark or troublesome – yet extremely important – than that of public acceptance" (Kasperson and Ram 2013:91).*

Yet acceptance is also the most difficult prerequisite to fulfill during changes in complicated technologies, non-transparent markets and regulatory settings. Even if acceptance is gained, this does not necessarily lead to the active involvement of citizens, it may result in passive tolerance only. Moreover, in cases where issues of acceptance arise, the situation usually gets more and more complex, as positive and negative consequences, interests, motives and values, as well as potential alternatives, tend to become more visible to the participants. While this 'transparency' is a vital necessity for democratic legitimation, everyday social life does in fact need a certain amount of 'voluntary blindness', i.e. the reduction of complexity 'to get things done'. Furthermore, acceptance is supposed to be result of extraordinary social exercises such as participation, be it via public hearings, mediation, or other forms. While these efforts are necessary to resolve conflicts, they are by no means routine. In Germany, we frequently observe conflicts over large infrastructure projects (like airports or large train stations) that result in such exercises. However, there is not always a need for public consent, such as every time people use public transport.

Nonetheless, for a positive outcome of the GEST, the overall population must develop some kind of attitude which stimulates action. The alternative strategy is to rely on the mechanisms of trust and distrust. Trust is a social mechanism for enabling action. Trust 'neutralizes' dangers which cannot be removed, but which should not disrupt actions. Trust is necessary in situations where somebody needs to assess how others will perform, before it is possible to monitor their actual performance (Gambetta 2008:217). We need to 'trust in trust' in order to enter situations which we cannot control, but which offer opportunities. Therefore, trust widens the scope of possible actions. However, it is the genuine quality of trust that makes it fragile: "Trust has the circular, self-presupposing and confirming character" (Luhmann 1995:129).

Trust-building costs time and effort. On the other hand, minor incidents let trust crumble and turn into distrust. Moreover, as trust is a self-referential commodity (Gambetta 2008), it cannot be enforced easily. Advertising for trust raises suspicion and is generally seen as hardly authentic (Japp 2010). Distrust, then, leads to the search for alternatives to avoid the situation, or to precautionary measures, i.e. additional support, if the distrusting actor cannot avoid involvement.

A final implication concerns trust/ distrust in *persons*, rather than trust/ distrust in *systems* (i.e. the services, structures, or institutions involved):

"Social evolution which achieves increasingly complex societies may in fact generate systems which require more confidence as prerequisite of participation and more trust as a condition of the best utilization of chances and opportunities" (Luhmann 1988a:99).

(Dis-)Trust in the Energy System

Attitudes towards complex and abstract systems for the provision of services are determined by experience with the reliability of the service outputs and with malfunctions, accidents or catastrophes, but also through the observation of symbolic references to the system, such as technical installations or familiar representatives of organizations (Stadtwerke).

Experience with infrastructure systems varies drastically from region to region, and from case to case. Overall, confidence in the reliability of electricity supply has been struck by setbacks in the USA (Kasperson and Ram 2013), while the confidence among the German population may, in the near future, be overstretched because barely anyone is prepared for a prolonged interruption of service as a result of lacking experience (Petermann et al. 2011:238).

A series of accidents – from Three Mile Island to Chernobyl, and, recently, Fukushima[62] – may have shaken the overall confidence in the technological branch of nuclear power generation. Fukushima has been depicted again and again as triggering the GEST.[63] Negative experiences encourage people to search for responsible actors, i.e. those towards whom trust had been addressed, and to decide whether such trust is warranted in the future. When a citizen's sense of trust has crumbled, several potential addresses of blame come to mind, such as private companies, the public administration and the government.

Shortly after the accident in Fukushima, several newspaper reports were published about the systematic, non-legitimate relationships between members of national nuclear regulatory regimes and the nuclear industry. Some researchers suspect that the revelation of such corruption leads to the (short-term) erosion of public trust (Tanter 2013) and that such a potential key incident remains 'stuck' in the public memory. Trust issues are triggered by key incidents and, moreover, by *processes of attribution* for who is responsible (or who is to blame) and the processes of decision-making on how to continue the trust relationship.

Although decisive trust indicators in public crises constitute symbolic references, the energy system is largely invisible, with the exception of visible infrastructure (pylons, plants etc.).

> *"[It is a] naturalized background, as ordinary and unremarkable to us as trees, daylight, and dirt" (Edwards 2004:185).*

---

[62] For the consequences of the Fukushima accident see (Khazai, Daniell, and Wenzel 2011)

[63] A claim worth challenging because of the many influential developments preceding this event; see (Bruns et al. 2010).

In our 'normal mode' we suppress any thought of the energy system, until it 'reappears' after accidents or failures. Infrastructure systems which require more direct interaction than the energy system are usually more susceptible to the influence of symbols: For example, on my first trip to Japan I marveled at the public transport system with brilliant ticket vending machines, impressive train technology and accurate punctuality, despite millions of daily travelers. I particularly noticed the formal behavior of the train personnel: The conductors wear uniform; they greet each other in military stile on shift exchange, then hold the door for the conductor all the while bowing down to show respect for the colleague. This little scene – everyday behavior for all involved – has symbolic value; it induced a great deal of confidence on my part and I deduced that the personnel apparently takes its responsibilities very seriously, enabling customers to trustingly commit themselves to use the transportation service although they are, for a determined period of time, physically exposed to the conducting skills of strangers.

Once current visions become incorporated into the future energy system, the role of the general public will change. More members of the public will cease to be a passive 'audience' which obtains electricity services; they will become active 'entrepreneurs' contributing to service provision. This new role assumes that actors develop a positive attitude towards unfamiliar technology, non-transparent markets and abstract regimes. The required positive attitude is composed of 'confidence' and 'trust'. Confidence is an attitude which helps ignore the limits, constraints, or dangers in situations where someone is not capable of influencing the social environment with his/ her own actions.

In Germany, people are confident that energy will be available tomorrow, despite their awareness of scenarios from science *and* fiction about possibilities of infrastructure breakdowns and bottlenecks. Most people are not prepared to live without energy for a longer period of time (Fekete

2011:15). Lack of confidence, on the other hand, can lead to a search for autonomy from energy system services. Diminishing confidence in technical services is exemplified by the growing Preppers movements in the USA and in Europe. Diminished confidence in turn leads to distrust of other persons, i.e. of governmental agencies, and trust is reserved only for one's own ability to prepare or to be prepared. However, we can find more modest examples. In recent years, less extreme cases of large-scale distrust have occurred, such as the generalized rejection of biofuel in Germany (E10) and, in the case of EHEC, of vegetables.

While distrust nonetheless triggers action, lack of trust will usually hinder action. For example, distrust led to opposition against 'smart meters' in private homes. The fear of data abuse by unauthorized agents contributed to a shift in Dutch energy policy:

> *"The mandatory acceptance of the meter for consumers [has been shifted] into voluntary acceptance" (Hoenkamp and Huitema 2012:2).*

The paradox formulation of this citation indicates the sociological problem at hand: Future energy systems are dependent on voluntary participation in terms of investments in energy technology and/ or 'smart use' of electricity. While overconfidence ('blind trust') can lead to excessive risk-taking, i.e. carelessness, a 'healthy distrust', confidence in the overall energy system transformation, and particular trusting actions are prerequisites for active involvement. Both, trust and confidence, systematically reinforce one other, and only if a certain threshold of trust and confidence is present, do people commit themselves to participate actively in the overall process (Kasperson and Ram 2013:95).

Governance of Trust

The idea of 'Governance of Trust' can assemble and reunite certain pointers for further research. First of all, thinking about trust and confidence in systems leads to the question of 'access points' which can enable operators, investors, consumers, etc. to attribute trust/ distrust. In this regard, the concept of an "architecture of trust" (Strulik 2007) is promising. For the abstract and mostly invisible energy system, an extensive architecture contributes to trust relationships in all three dimensions (structural, institutional and operational). In all three cases, the concept of an 'architecture of trust' provides a setting for varying addresses of trust attribution.

(6) In the structural dimension, trust relationships can be addressed towards material objects (e.g. infrastructures) and towards organizations (e.g. large companies and local cooperatives (*Energie-Genossenschaften*)).
(7) In the institutional dimension, trust relationships can be based on shared rules, values and roles.
(8) In the operational dimension, trust can be attributed to different time frames for maintaining the service in the present (experience), to the ongoing transformation process (programs which are scientific, technical and political), or even to future states (visions and expectation statements).

In addition, the architecture of trust affects the validity and intensity of thresholds of trust/ distrust: How much information retrieval do actors perform before taking a trusting decision and, simultaneously, how much ignorance are actors prepared to tolerate?

Tentatively, we can identify well-known or novel addresses of trust:

- Trust/ distrust in black boxes like 'autonomous, smart and intelligent' agents can raise questions on the appropriate level of delegation of control.
- Trust/ distrust in agreements about responsibility for participation in virtual power plants and in decentralized networks.
- Trust/ distrust towards persons/ roles, organizations and their decision programs which refer to different functional domains in society, for example private enterprises which comprise economic (infrastructure-investments) as well as legal, political (lobbyism), or scientific (applied, industrial research) activities.
- Trust and distrust in institutionalized regimes.

Certainly, trust cannot be enforced or successfully subjected to advertising. The buildup of trust takes a long time. Yet the corrosion of trust takes only minor occurrences. Thus recognizing the necessity of trust and confidence in the future energy system constitutes only a first step, whilst elaborating on the conditions on how trust can be developed is the next step.

References

Amin, M. 2001. "Toward Self-Healing Energy Infrastructure Systems." *IEEE Computer Applications in Power* 14(1):20–28.

Bruns, Elke, Dörte Ohlhorst, Bernd Wenzel, and Johann Köppel. 2010. *Renewable Energies in Germany's Electricity Market: A Biography of the Innovation Process*. Dordrecht [et al.]: Springer.

Brunsson, Nils. 2007. *The Consequences of Decision-Making*. Oxford, New York: Oxford University Press.

Depuru, S. S. S. R., L. Wang, and V. Devabhaktuni. 2011. "Smart Meters for Power Grid: Challenges, Issues, Advantages and Status." *Renewable and Sustainable Energy Reviews* 15(6):2736–42.

Edwards, Paul N. 2004. "Infrastructure and Modernity: Force, Time, and Social Organization in the History of Socio-Technical Systems." Pp. 185–225 in *Modernity and Technology*, edited by Thomas Misa, Philip Brey, and Andrew Feenberg. Cambridge, London: MIT Press.

Edwards, Paul N., Steven J. Jackson, Geoffrey C. Bowker, and Cory P. Knobel. 2007. *Understanding Infrastructure: Dynamics, Tensions, and Design*. Ann Arbor: DeepBlue. Retrieved (http://deepblue.lib.umich.edu/handle/2027.42/49353).

Fekete, Alexander. 2011. "Common Criteria for the Assessment of Critical Infrastructures." *International Journal of Disaster Risk Science* 2(1):15–24.

Fuenfschilling, Lea and Bernhard Truffer. 2014. "The Structuration of Socio-Technical Regimes – Conceptual Foundations from Institutional Theory." *Research Policy*. Retrieved January 30, 2014 (http://www.sciencedirect.com/science/article/pii/S0048733313001893).

Gambetta, Diego. 2008. "Can We Trust Trust?" Pp. 213–37 in *Trust. Making and Breaking Cooperative Relations*, edited by Diego Gambetta. Oxford: Basil Blackwell.

Geels, Frank W. 2014. "Regime Resistance against Low-Carbon Transitions: Introducing Politics and Power into the Multi-Level Perspective." *Theory, Culture & Society* 0263276414531627.

Geels, F. W. 2004. "From Sectoral Systems of Innovation to Socio-Technical Systems: Insights about Dynamics and Change from Sociology and Institutional Theory." *Research Policy* 33(6-7):897–920.

Grin, John, Jan Rotmans, and Johan Schot. 2010. *Transitions to Sustainable Development: New Directions in the Study of Long Term Transformative Change*. New York/London: Routledge. Retrieved July 17, 2013 (http://dare.uva.nl/en/record/395230).

Gross, Matthias and Rüdiger Mautz. 2015. *Renewable Energies*. London, New York: Routledge.

Hoenkamp, R. A. and G. B. Huitema. 2012. "Good Standards for Smart Meters." Pp. 1–6 in *European Energy Market (EEM), 2012 9th International Conference on the*. Retrieved (http://ieeexplore.ieee.org/xpl/articleDetails.jsp?arnumber=6254820).

Kasperson, Roger E. and Bonnie J. Ram. 2013. "The Public Acceptance of New Energy Technologies." *Daedalus* 142(1):90–96.

Khazai, Bijan, James E. Daniell, and Friedemann Wenzel. 2011. "The March 2011 Japan Earthquake – Analysis of Losses, Impacts, and Implications for the Understanding of Risks Posed by Extreme Events." *TATuP* 20(3):22–33.

Kröger, Wolfgang and Enrico Zio. 2011. *Vulnerable Systems*. London, Dordrecht, Heidelberg, New York: Springer.

Luhmann, Niklas. 1988. "Familiarity, Confidence, Trust: Problems and Alternatives." Pp. 94–107 in *Trust. Making and Breaking Cooperative Relations*, edited by Diego Gambetta. Oxford: Basil Blackwell.

Luhmann, Niklas. 1995. *Social Systems*. Stanford, California: Stanford University Press.

Mayntz, Renate. 2009. "The Changing Governance of Large Technical Infrastructure Systems." Pp. 121–50 in Über Governance. Institutionen und Prozesse politischer Regelung, Schriften aus dem Max-Planck-Institut für Gesellschaftsforschung, Band 62. Frankfurt am Main, New York: Campus.

Ma, Y., L. Zhou, N. Tse, A. Osman, and L. L. Lai. 2009. "An Initial Study on Computational Intelligence for Smart Grid." Pp. 3425–29 in *Proceedings of the 2009 International Conference on Machine Learning and Cybernetics*, vol. 6. Retrieved (http://www.scopus.com/inward/record.url?eid=2-s2.0-70350710179&partnerID=40&md5=7a2e0f982e073385f919cf5fe0ebeef3).

Perrow, Charles. 2011. "Software Failures, Security, and Cyberattacks." *TATuP* 20(3):41–46.

Petermann, Thomas, Harald Bradke, Arne Lüllmann, Maik Paetzsch, and Ulrich Riehm. 2011. *Was bei einem Blackout geschieht: Folgen eines langandauernden und großflächigen Stromausfalls*. Berlin: edition sigma.

Ramchurn, S., P. Vytelingum, A. Rogers, and N. Jennings. 2012. "Putting the' Smarts' into the Smart Grid: A Grand Challenge for Artificial Intelligence." *Communications of the ACM* 55(4):86–97.

Smith, Adrian, Andy Stirling, and Frans Berkhout. 2005. "The Governance of Sustainable Socio-Technical Transitions." *Research Policy* 34(10):1491–1510.

Strulik, Torsten. 2007. "Rating Agencies, Ignorance and the Production of System Trust." Pp. 239–58 in *Towards a cognitive mode in global finance. The Governance of a Knowledge-based Financial Systems*, edited by Torsten Strulik and Helmut Willke. Frankfurt am Main, New York: Campus. Retrieved December 3, 2012 (http://pub.uni-bielefeld.de/publication/1862297).

Strunz, Sebastian. 2014. "The German Energy Transition as a Regime Shift." *Ecological Economics* 100:150–58.

Tanter, Richard. 2013. "After Fukushima: A Survey of Corruption in the Global Nuclear Power Industry." *Asian Perspective* 37(4):475–500.

Weber, K. Matthias and Harald Rohracher. 2012. "Legitimizing Research, Technology and Innovation Policies for Transformative Change: Combining Insights from Innovation Systems and Multi-Level Perspective in a Comprehensive 'Failures' Framework." *Research Policy* 41(6):1037–47.

Implementing Technology Assessment through Stakeholder Platforms: Strategic Resource Logistics for Socially Robust Models of Sustainability Innovation

Masaru Yarime[64]

Abstract

To address global problems of sustainability, which are often ill-defined and intermingled, it is necessary for us to achieve a scientific understanding of the complex and dynamic interaction between natural and human systems and the steps taken by society to attain sustainability innovation. To do this, we need to integrate knowledge from various academic disciplines in the natural sciences, social sciences, and humanities effectively and efficiently. Considering the significant degree of diversity and uncertainty involved, a major challenge is determining how to organize and implement serious participation and fruitful collaboration between academia and stakeholders, including industry, the government, and civil society. This will require careful consideration of the types of joint initiatives and networking suitable to contribute to identifying desirable goals and targets and to developing complementary skills and capacities, of the mechanisms and stakeholder relations that

---

64 Science, Technology, and Innovation Governance (STIG), Graduate School of Public Policy, University of Tokyo, Japan; and Department of Science, Technology, Engineering and Public Policy (STEaPP), University College London, United Kingdom. Email: yarimemasa@gmail.com

have been put in place to drive practices and initiatives, and of the factors that promote or obstruct their successful implementation. Considering the diversity of stakeholders in terms of their perceptions, motivations, and behavior dependent upon economic, social, and historical contexts, a key for creating knowledge, designing targets, and implementing processes for innovation would be the creation and management of stakeholder platforms.

Technology assessment would be conducted concurrently with strategic resource logistics, in which collaboration with stakeholders is promoted for creating, sharing, and utilizing the relevant knowledge together in society so that feedback from them is well integrated into the process of technology assessment. This paper examines a case of innovation facilitated by the creation of stakeholder platforms for sustainable management of phosphorus. Participants were researchers and practitioners involved in the entire value chain ranging from exploration and mining to processing, transport, use, and recycling. The lessons to be learned from facilitating the sharing of knowledge and expertise by stakeholders by means of strategic resource logistics would contribute to establishing socially robust models of sustainability innovation.

Introduction

Sustainable phosphorus management concerns the supply chain from the point where phosphorus-containing waste has been produced by humans, livestock, and industry. While dissipation refers to the intended or unintended loss of phosphorus in mining, processing, and use, recycling covers the processing, marketing, and use of recycled waste products. One of the critical challenges for sustainable phosphorus management is to make phosphorus recovery economical, reliable, and predictable, while ensuring that the use of recycled phosphorus products does not have an adverse impact on health or the environment. It is therefore crucial to manage phosphorus stocks and flows using a systems approach, linking exploration, mining, processing, use, dissipation, and recycling (Matsubae-Yokoyama, Kubo, Nakajima, and Nagasaka, 2009; Matsubae, Kajiyama, Hiraki, and Nagasaka, 2011).

Particular attention needs to be paid to the current and potential markets, quality, and price of products, costs of production processes, the available and future forms of technology, institutional structures, and public perception and behavior. The stakeholders involved are diverse, including industries creating waste streams and others focusing on phosphorus recovery and include farmers, governmental regulatory and specialized agencies, public environmental and health organizations, researchers in academia, and agricultural and health non-governmental organizations (NGOs). It is very important to give a comprehensive and structured overview of the current state of our knowledge and to identify and major gaps in research.

To address this challenge, Global TraPs (Transdisciplinary Processes for Sustainable Phosphorus Management) has been initiated as a multistakeholder project on the sustainable management of the global phosphorus cycle and involves academia, industry, and the public sector (Yarime, Carliell-Marquet, Lang, Le, Malley, Matsubae, Matsuo, Ohtake, Omlin, Petzet, Scholz, Shiroyama, Ulrich, and Watts, 2014). We examine the potential for recycling phosphorus from a variety of waste sources as well as for preventing phosphorus dissipation by establishing socially robust business models integrating innovative technologies, business strategies, and public policies. Sustainable phosphorus management is explored using an integrated approach combining technological, management, and policy perspectives (Yarime, 2010).

Among the questions to be addressed are:

- What are the technological challenges for reducing costs and improving the quality of recycled phosphorus?
- How ca a system for the effective and efficient matching of supply and demand for recycled phosphorus be established?
- What similarities and differences can be identified in phosphorus recycling between different sectors, including agriculture and manufacturing?

While there is a large potential for recycling phosphorus from different sources, only a small portion of the secondary phosphorus resources has been utilized so far. As the supply chain of phosphorus ranges from exploration, mining, and transportation to its use and recycling, it is of critical importance to establish a system for collecting, sharing, and utilizing a large amount of data and coordinating the behavior of the relevant stakeholders involved in the different stages of resource flows.

The creation and management of stakeholder platforms would be a key for cocreating knowledge, codesigning targets, and coimplementing processes for a sustainability transition. In Japan the Phosphorus Recycling Promotion Council has been established recently with experts from academia, industry, and the government to design and implement national strategies for socially robust phosphorus recycling systems. In Europe, the Nutrient Platform has been initiated in the Netherlands, together with private companies, knowledge institutes, government authorities, and NGOs agreeing to share and utilize any relevant knowledge. In this paper a preliminary analysis is conducted to examine the mechanisms for establishing stakeholder platforms in different contexts. Particular attention is given to understanding how to design and implement a system facilitating serious participation and fruitful collaboration among stakeholders, what types of joint initiatives and networking contribute to identifying desirable goals and targets and to developing complementary skills and capacities, and what factors promote or obstruct their successful implementation. Also discussed are the implications for establishing a system for sustainable phosphorus management on the basis of global cooperation.

Challenge of Sustainable Phosphorus Management

An essential first step toward the sustainable management of phosphorus is the mapping of the direct and indirect demands for phosphorus in an economy. For example, the substance flows of phosphorus in the Japanese economy are estimated to be 618 kt (Matsubae, Kajiyama, Hiraki, and Nagasaka, 2011). Approximately 284 kt of phosphorus is employed annually at farms and ranches in the form of fertilizer, one of the largest input flows in the entire domestic phosphorus flow. The values of input flows to the food and feed sectors are also large, mainly from world imports and marine resources (163.1 kt) and the domestic crop production from farmlands (45.2 kt), with the phosphorus mainly being consumed by humans and livestock (97.6 kt and 111.0 kt). Livestock grows by eating grass and feed on ranches, and the phosphorus in livestock manure ends up accumulating in the soil, the amount of which (285.3 kt) is nearly equal to that from fertilizer at farms and ranches. Another main output is the human waste that ends up flowing down rivers, in the ocean, or in landfill. In addition, 110.5 kt of phosphorus is associated with the steel industry as mineral resources, most of which is condensed in slag from steelmaking.

There are a variety of potential phosphorus resources within the Japanese economy, including food waste, sewage sludge, steelmaking slag, and other industrial wastes, totaling approximately 240 kt per year, which is comparable to the amount of phosphorus used annually in fertilizer of approximately 284 kt. Hence, an appropriate nationwide recycling strategy could potentially provide the majority of phosphorus required for agricultural production in the country. Sustainable phosphorus management is also of economic importance. While the size of the domestic fertilizer market is only five billion U.S. dollars per year, it supports all the food-related industries and businesses in the country, whose total sales reach 800 billion U.S. dollars.

In the vegetation process, fertilizer is used for plant growth. Not all the phosphorus in fertilizer, however, is transformed into the harvested products, as loss is caused by absorption in the pedosphere, diffusion into the hydrosphere, and waste in residual portions of agricultural products. Substance flow analysis focusing on the phosphorus contained in products tends to neglect such phosphorus flows. As a new indicator for considering the direct and indirect phosphorus requirements of society, the virtual phosphorus ore requirement (VPOR) has been proposed (Matsubae, Kajiyama, Hiraki, and Nagasaka, 2011). As in the case of virtual water (Hoekstra and Chapagain, 2007), estimation of VPOR requires that hidden phosphorus flows be taken into consideration, which constitute the total phosphorus requirement excluding the amount contained in agricultural products and including the loss to the environment, nonedible parts, and feedstuff for livestock.

The characteristics of current phosphorus management practices and approaches in different sectors are diverse with regard to the temporal and spatial scales of the issue; technological measures, including the types of technology, energy consumption, costs of investment and operation; key stakeholders involved, such as farmers, industry, consumers, and public sectors; and institutional conditions, including public policies and interventions. A solid understanding of the factors influencing phosphorus dissipation and recycling in different domains will be necessary to achieve sustainable phosphorus management. Potentially there are three main areas for implementing phosphorus recycling: recycling of the phosphorus contained in food and feed; recycling that from wastewater; and recycling that from industries that use high-quality phosphate (Ohtake, 2010).

Recognizing the significance and potential of phosphorus recycling, some experts and practitioners have started to pay attention to the development of phosphorus management and recycling as a new green industry. The active involvement of industry, however, is still limited, and there are not many cases in which phosphorus recycling has been successfully implemented in practice. At the current stage of development, the recycling of phosphorus is not a feasible business opportunity, as the conventional practice of buying normal fertilizers while wasting water and sludge is much cheaper. The recycling of phosphorus, therefore, has not yet become a strategic issue for major companies in the chemical industry. One of the critical issues which we need to tackle is how to establish socially robust business models in a broader sense, integrating scientific understanding, technological development, corporate strategies, and public policies, for a successful implementation of phosphorus recycling.

Roles and Functions of the Transdisciplinary Process

In the transdisciplinary process, a crucial step toward jointly defining the problem and conducting transdisciplinary case studies is to build partnerships among key stakeholders (Scholz, 2011). Relevant actors in academia, industry, government, and NGOs need to be involved in identifying the critical challenges (Yarime, Trencher, Mino, Scholz, Olsson, Ness, Frantzeskaki, and Rotmans, 2012). While the need for phosphorus recovery has been identified as an important issue by various institutions, the actions taken by stakeholders around the world continue to be limited. In designing a phosphorus recycling system, it is necessary to approach this issue at multiple levels, including local, national, and global levels (Shiroyama, Yarime, Matsuo, Schroeder, Scholz, and Ulrich, 2012).

While the recycling system would depend very much on the local characteristics and context, it would also be influenced by national resource management strategies and institutional frameworks. Generally speaking, the recycling of phosphorus is not yet considered to be a high priority issue at the national level, except in a few countries such as Sweden, where a target is set to recover 60% of phosphorus from sewages by 2015. A full commitment to implementing phosphorus recycling has not yet been made by industry, which is increasingly influenced by the business environment in the global economy.

Many actors in different sectors have stakes in recycling phosphorus. Phosphorus can be characterized as an essential, nonsubstitutable, but low-cost commodity that each person consumes, as well as a source of environmental pollution. It is crucial to identify who has what kind of a stake within the system and to find the best way to realize a situation in which a common solution is found for satisfying different interests and objectives (Shiroyama, Yarime, Matsuo, Schroeder, Scholz, and Ulrich, 2012). For instance, close collaboration between cement companies, fertilizer companies, and the local government can be a potential source for implementing phosphorus recycling. The sewage department of a local government has to extract phosphorus to meet the water quality standard to avoid environmental degradation. Fertilizer companies need phosphorus for producing fertilizer, and cement companies require the level of phosphorus contained in sludge to be low because sludge with a high concentration of phosphorus can weaken the strength of the product (Ohtake, 2011).

Currently one of the most serious challenges to the recycling of phosphorus is how to expand the market for recycled phosphorus. For this purpose it is very important to maintain the stability of supply and the quality of products utilizing recycled phosphorus. Institutional measures to accelerate the closing of the phosphorus chain would include implementation of phosphorus discharge criteria in waste stream regulations and revision of lengthy and cost-intensive permission procedures and requirements for recovery technologies (Drizo, 2012).

We then need to prepare for sustainable transitions by exploring feasible strategies for social business models, with the relevant stakeholders being closely involved. To do this, we could consider pursuing consensus at two levels. The first one is whether we should go for a soft or detransformation of sewage and wastes. While there has been concern about heavy metals, new chemicals, pathogens, and other biological issues, it is not completely clear whether a kind of soft processing including organic matter might be a better option than incineration. This type of consensus building could take place in a precompetitive arena, although it might also affect industrial competition at a later stage.

Creation of Stakeholder Platforms in Japan and Europe

A preliminary analysis is conducted to examine the emerging examples of the successful implementation of the recycling of phosphorus in Japan and Europe. In Japan, for example, phosphorus recycling in the sewage treatment plant in Gifu, Japan, has been in operation since 2010, and the fertilizer utilizing recycled phosphorus has been sold to farmers.

Where phosphorus removal is performed in sewage works, sludge mono-incineration ash contains phosphorus at concentrations similar to those of rock phosphate. A full-scale plant for phosphorus recovery from sludge incineration ash has recently started operation at Gifu city in Japan (Goto, 2009). The full-scale plant is now making a great contribution to the sustainability of local agriculture because the quality of the recovered phosphorus matches the local demand very well. There are critical challenges, however, including the high capital cost for plant construction and the difficulty in establishing stable channels for the distribution and sale of recycled phosphorus, which might discourage the expanded use of this technology.

In Europe, a couple of companies which previously operated in the field of detergents are now utilizing their extensive knowledge of phosphorus for different types of purification and reprocessing. Ostara is running five plants for recycling phorphorus in Europe. Companies such as Thermphos, Prayon, and ICL have already joined the Global TraPs project. The development and implementation of innovative technologies is currently being explored in Germany, and recovery measures in the water sector and from manure have started being introduced in the U.K.

The knowledge generated in the transdisciplinary process is expected to be used by practitioners in their business and policy decisions for achieving a sustainable use of phosphorus, which demands cooperation and coordination across different sectors. Close collaboration among relevant stakeholders including academia, industry, and the public sector is urgently required in order to cope with this critical challenge (Yarime, Trencher, Mino, Scholz, Olsson, Ness, Frantzeskaki, and Rotmans, 2012). As an attempt to address this, the Phosphorus Recycling Promotion Council of Japan (PRPCJ) was established in 2008 by inviting experts from academia, industry, and the public sector to participate. This nationwide association is supported by the four relevant ministries of the Japanese government and currently has approximately 140 members, including more than 70 corporate members. Based on the PRPCJ activities, a national platform for industry-academia-government collaboration was also initiated in 2011 to discuss and implement national strategies for robust phosphorus recycling systems.

In Europe, the Nutrient Platform was established in 2011 in the Netherlands, with more than twenty Dutch companies, knowledge institutes, government authorities and NGO's signing the Phosphate Value Chain Agreement (Dutch Nutrient Platform, 2011). The Nutrient Platform is a cross-sectoral network of Dutch organizations that share a common concern for the global impact of phosphorus depletion and the way society is dealing with nutrients in general. Together with the Dutch government, the Nutrient Platform intends to support organizations throughout the value chain in completing the phosphorus cycle. They all share the ambition of creating a sustainable market within two years, where as many reusable phosphate streams as possible will be returned to the cycle in an environmentally friendly way and where the recycled phosphate will be exported to the fullest extent possible, as long as a surplus exists in the Dutch market, in order to contribute elsewhere to soil improvement and food production. To achieve the vision and mission, the platform practices an approach of learning by doing within a framework of action learning and new types of partnerships.

The First European Sustainable Phosphorus Conference 2013 was held in Brussels in March 2013, with the purpose of raising awareness about the necessity of a more sustainable phosphate management within the context of a resource efficient Europe (European Phosphorus Platform, 2013). Its goal was to facilitate support for a clear and coherent legislative framework to create an enabling environment for eco-innovation, a sustainable European market for secondary phosphorus, and more efficient phosphorus use.

Different nutrient waste flows and market possibilities will be connected between stakeholders, including the private sector, knowledge institutes, government, and NGOs, to further develop sustainable nutrient chains within Europe. At the conference, participants reached a consensus to launch the European Phosphorus Platform in order to continue dialogues, raise awareness, and trigger action to address the phosphorus challenge, with significant implications for ensuring food security, geopolitical stability, and environmental sustainability.

In North America, a kickoff workshop was organized in May 2013 to launch the Research Coordination Network (RCN) in Washington, D.C. (Sustainable P Initiative, 2013). The workshop was meant to bring together some of the world's top scientists, engineers, and technical experts to spark an interdisciplinary synthesis of data, perspectives, and understanding about phosphorus to envision solutions for phosphorus sustainability.

Key stakeholders from relevant sectors shared their knowledge and expertise on various dimensions of the global phosphorus system, including farmers and growers, food processors, fertilizer producers, waste managers, water quality managers, regulators, and legislators. Two challenges were identified, namely phosphorus efficiency and phosphorus recycling. The RCN coordinating phosphorus research has been funded by the National Science Foundation to create a sustainable food system.

These experiences of establishing national or regional platforms involving key stakeholders will provide valuable lessons and implications for implementing phosphorus recycling successfully in different technological, economic, and institutional contexts.

Acknowledgement

This paper is written as part of our work in the ENERGY-TRANS Alliance financed by the Helmholtz-Association in Germany. I am grateful for hints to improve the arguments by Patrick Sumpf. Moreover, I am thankful for the editing work by Mira Klemm who improved the readability of the text considerably.

References

Amin, M. 2001. "Toward Self-Healing Energy Infrastructure Systems." *IEEE Computer Applications in Power* 14(1):20–28.

Bruns, Elke, Dörte Ohlhorst, Bernd Wenzel, and Johann Köppel. 2010. *Renewable Energies in Germany's Electricity Market: A Biography of the Innovation Process*. Dordrecht [et al.]: Springer.

Brunsson, Nils. 2007. *The Consequences of Decision-Making*. Oxford, New York: Oxford University Press.

Depuru, Soma S. S. R., L. Wang, and V. Devabhaktuni. 2011. "Smart Meters for Power Grid: Challenges, Issues, Advantages and Status." *Renewable and Sustainable Energy Reviews* 15(6):2736–42.

Edwards, Paul N. 2004. "Infrastructure and Modernity: Force, Time, and Social Organization in the History of Socio-Technical Systems." Pp. 185–225 in *Modernity and Technology*, edited by T. Misa, P. Brey, and A. Feenberg. Cambridge, London: MIT Press.

Edwards, Paul N., Steven J. Jackson, Geoffrey C. Bowker, and Cory P. Knobel. 2007. *Understanding Infrastructure: Dynamics, Tensions, and Design*. Ann Arbor: DeepBlue. Retrieved (http://deepblue.lib.umich.edu/handle/2027.42/49353).

Fekete, Alexander. 2011. "Common Criteria for the Assessment of Critical Infrastructures." *International Journal of Disaster Risk Science* 2(1):15–24.

Fuenfschilling, Lea and Bernhard Truffer. 2014. "The Structuration of Socio-Technical Regimes – Conceptual Foundations from Institutional Theory." *Research Policy*.

Gambetta, Diego. 2008. "Can We Trust Trust?" Pp. 213–37 in *Trust. Making and Breaking Cooperative Relations*, edited by D. Gambetta. Oxford [u.a.]: Basil Blackwell.

Geels, Frank W. 2014. "Regime Resistance against Low-Carbon Transitions: Introducing Politics and Power into the Multi-Level Perspective." *Theory, Culture & Society* 1–20.

Geels, F. W. 2004. "From Sectoral Systems of Innovation to Socio-Technical Systems: Insights about Dynamics and Change from Sociology and Institutional Theory." *Research Policy* 33(6-7):897–920.

Grin, John, Jan Rotmans, and Johan Schot. 2010. *Transitions to Sustainable Development: New Directions in the Study of Long Term Transformative Change*. New York/London: Routledge. Retrieved July 17, 2013 (http://dare.uva.nl/en/record/395230).

Gross, Matthias and Rüdiger Mautz. 2015. *Renewable Energies*. London, New York: Routledge.

Hoenkamp, R. A. and G. B. Huitema. 2012. "Good Standards for Smart Meters." Pp. 1–6 in *European Energy Market (EEM), 2012 9th International Conference on the*. Retrieved March 14, 2014 (http://ieeexplore.ieee.org/xpl/articleDetails.jsp?arnumber=6254820).

Hughes, T. P. 1986. "The Seamless Web: Technology, Science, Etcetera, Etcetera." *Social Studies of Science* 16(2):281–92.

Japp, Klaus P. 2010. "Risiko Und Gefahr. Zum Problem Authentischer Kommunikation." Pp. 281–308 in *Ökologische Aufklärung. 25 Jahre "Ökologische Kommunikation"*, edited by C. Büscher and K. P. Japp. Wiesbaden: VS Verlag.

Kasperson, Roger E. and Bonnie J. Ram. 2013. "The Public Acceptance of New Energy Technologies." *Daedalus* 142(1):90–96.

Khazai, Bijan, James E. Daniell, and Friedemann Wenzel. 2011. "The March 2011 Japan Earthquake – Analysis of Losses, Impacts, and Implications for the Understanding of Risks Posed by Extreme Events." *TATuP* 20(3):22–33.

Kröger, Wolfgang and Enrico Zio. 2011. *Vulnerable Systems*. London, Dordrecht, Heidelberg, New York: Springer.

Künneke, Rolf W. 2008. "Institutional Reform and Technological Practise: The Case of Electricity." *Industrial and Corporate Change* 17(2):233–65.

Luhmann, Niklas. 1988a. "Familiarity, Confidence, Trust: Problems and Alternatives." Pp. 94–107 in *Trust. Making and Breaking Cooperative Relations*, edited by D. Gambetta. Oxford [u.a.]: Basil Blackwell.

Luhmann, Niklas. 1988b. "Organisation." Pp. 165–85 in *Mikropolitik*, edited by W. Küpper and G. Ortmann. Opladen: Westdeutscher Verlag.

Luhmann, Niklas. 1995. *Social Systems*. Stanford, California: Stanford University Press.

Mayntz, Renate. 2009. "The Changing Governance of Large Technical Infrastructure Systems." Pp. 121–50 in Über Governance. Institutionen und Prozesse politischer Regelung, Schriften aus dem Max-Planck-Institut für Gesellschaftsforschung, Band 62. Frankfurt am Main, New York: Campus.

Ma, Y., L. Zhou, N. Tse, A. Osman, and L. L. Lai. 2009. "An Initial Study on Computational Intelligence for Smart Grid." Pp. 3425–29 in *Proceedings of the 2009 International Conference on Machine Learning and Cybernetics*, vol. 6. Retrieved March 1, 2014 (http://www.scopus.com/inward/record.url?eid=2-s2.0-70350710179&partnerID=40&md5=7a2e0f982e073385f919cf5fe0ebeef3).

Perrow, Charles. 2011. "Software Failures, Security, and Cyberattacks." *TATuP* 20(3):41–46.

Petermann, Thomas, Harald Bradke, Arne Lüllmann, Maik Paetzsch, and Ulrich Riehm. 2011. *Was bei einem Blackout geschieht: Folgen eines langandauernden und großflächigen Stromausfalls*. Berlin: edition sigma.

Ramchurn, S., P. Vytelingum, A. Rogers, and N. Jennings. 2012. "Putting the 'Smarts' into the Smart Grid: A Grand Challenge for Artificial Intelligence." *Communications of the ACM* 55(4):86–97.

Smith, Adrian, Andy Stirling, and Frans Berkhout. 2005. "The Governance of Sustainable Socio-Technical Transitions." *Research Policy* 34(10):1491–1510.

Strulik, Torsten. 2007. "Rating Agencies, Ignorance and the Production of System Trust." Pp. 239–58 in *Towards a Cognitive Mode in Global Finance. The Governance of a Knowledge-based Financial Systems*, edited by T. Strulik and H. Willke. Frankfurt am Main, New York: Campus.

Strunz, Sebastian. 2014. "The German Energy Transition as a Regime Shift." *Ecological Economics* 100:150–58.

Tanter, Richard. 2013. "After Fukushima: A Survey of Corruption in the Global Nuclear Power Industry." *Asian Perspective* 37(4):475–500.

Weber, K. Matthias and Harald Rohracher. 2012. "Legitimizing Research, Technology and Innovation Policies for Transformative

Change: Combining Insights from Innovation Systems and Multi-Level Perspective in a Comprehensive 'Failures' Framework." *Research Policy* 41(6):1037–47.

Technology Provider and Receiver Interactions: The Capability Threshold Concept and Its Application to Technology Assessment

Shingo Kano

Background

There are very broad definitions of technology assessment (TA), such as those provided by Coates (1976), Porter (1995) and Decker (2004). These definitions commonly pointed out that TA includes policy and social studies and multiple dimensions of technological analysis from the viewpoint of various stakeholders. Decker (2004) provides one typical explanation: "Technology assessment (TA) is a scientific, interactive and communicative process, which aims to contribute to the formation of public and political opinion on societal aspects of science and technology." Multidimensional analysis, however, easily leads to complexity, decreased accuracy, and tradeoffs between width and depth.

A common perspective of analysis across various stakeholders is required to avoid such complexity and eliminate the horizontal aspects of TA. The analysis should have a more narrow focus and the potential to generalize observations to other cases. This chapter focuses on a study of how a recognition gap occurs between an innovator and other stakeholders beginning from a more narrow focus on the recognition gap between innovators. Technology transfer, especially in university-industry relationships, represents a relationship between stakeholders who are highly technologically knowledgeable. The university as a technology provider and the firm as a technology receiver both have difficulty handling early stage technologies without a proof of concept. The constraints and limitations on these stakeholders serve as a good reference and control for the relationships with nontechnical stakeholders.

Generally, the more creative and original the university research, the fewer the researchers in this field who are able to recognize the value of the research and the lower the probability that a company has such personnel. Such research consequently exceeds the capacity for evaluation and cannot be absorbed through channels such as collaborative research and licensing. It is therefore difficult to evaluate ideas at an early stage of research, i.e., before acquiring a proof of concept in the process of technology transfer.

Cohen and Levinthal (1990) discussed the notion of "absorptive capacity," illustrating an organization's knowledge to create innovative capabilities and defining a firm's ability "to recognize the value of new, external knowledge; assimilate it; and apply it to commercial ends." Drawing on the view of a firm's dynamic capabilities, Zahra and George (2002) showed how absorptive capacity determines the gap between a firm's potential and its realized capacity to innovate.

Atkinson (1994) reported on a partial failure of traditional technology transfer at the Harvard Medical School based on a survey of disclosures and proposals for industry relationships from 1977 to 1980. He explained it as follows:

"While a significant portion of these were appropriate for traditional patenting and licensing, a pattern emerged for a select category of projects for which that approach was ineffective. These projects were based on seminal technologies with the potential for broad applications – rather than leading to a single product, they might lead to a class of new diagnostics or therapeutics. Despite their patentability and power, however, they rarely attracted serious interest from established pharmaceutical firms until at least three to five years after initial disclosure."(Atkinson, 1994)

This case explains the phenomenon wherein, within a specific situation, an emerging new technology falls into the development gap, for which a university spin-off company is needed to serve as a technology bridging vehicle to facilitate industrialization. Atkinson (1994) commented that this was the reason Harvard University set up its university-affiliated venture capital fund. The implication is that technology transfer depends both on the nature of the technology and the receiver's capabilities. The point of departure is the recognition gap between university and company research. At the heart of a firm's technology transfer problems is the question of how to deal with that gap.

To illustrate these gaps between technology providers and receivers, Kano (2001) proposed the concept of the *technology-transfer effective frontier* to define the forms of technology transfer. With some generalization and modifications, this gap analysis framework can be applied to other TA stakeholders.

The purpose of this chapter is to introduce an analytical framework for technology transfer between innovators, and then expand this framework to apply to relationships between an innovator and other stakeholders to explain the recognition gap in TA.

The Concept of a Technology-Transfer Effective Frontier

University-industry relationships (UILs) typically involve a technology transfer process from one organization to the other, with activities covering simple licensing and collaboration accompanied by scientific and technological evaluations. Companies exhibit rational behavior in evaluating a university's research. First, a company will import technology from outside the firm if it is relevant to the firm's core businesses. Second, the firm must understand the content of the technology to effectively integrate it with its in-house technology. Those two components constitute the firm's absorptive capability.

If the research is at an embryonic stage, the firm will have difficulty determining its relevance to its businesses and understanding its scientific content. Therefore, the lower the maturity of the research, the higher the level of absorptive capability needed by the firm.

Figure 1 depicts this relationship, showing the maturity of academic research on the x-axis and the firm's required level of absorptive capacity on the y-axis. Given the stage of maturity of academic research, the level of absorptive capacity can be determined as a threshold value, below which a technology transfer is unlikely. These threshold values constitute a continuously decreasing function, called the *technology-transfer effective frontier*. In other words, the shaded region is the area where technology transfer occurs.

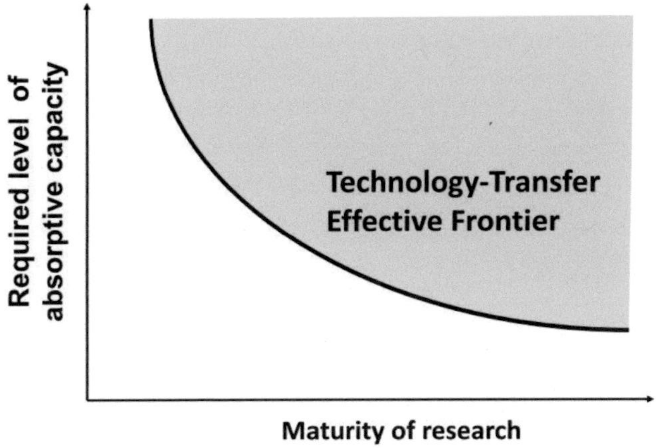

Figure 1: Technology-Transfer Effective Frontier

Recognition Gap and Bridging Paths

After establishing the technology transfer framework, it is possible to investigate why the gap exists. The limits to university research are defined by the maturity coordinates, beyond which research is no longer conducted in the academic institution. This concept is illustrated in Figure 2.

This limitation of university research can be drawn as a vertical straight line that intersects at the value of α in the x-axis. The shaded area surrounded by the line denoting the limit of university research and the technology-transfer effective frontier is the area where technology transfer from university to industry occurs.

Public-sector-funded basic research should be of a level of maturity lower than α. Those firms whose absorptive capacity is below β, which is the value of the y-axis value intersected by the value of α in the x-axis, cannot absorb the research even if the subject of the research is within the limits of their businesses.

Even if the university research progresses further, the collaboration between the university and the firm might never occur for research located below the technology-transfer effective frontier. This situation is the "recognition gap," and the distance toward the frontier can be used as the degree of the gap.

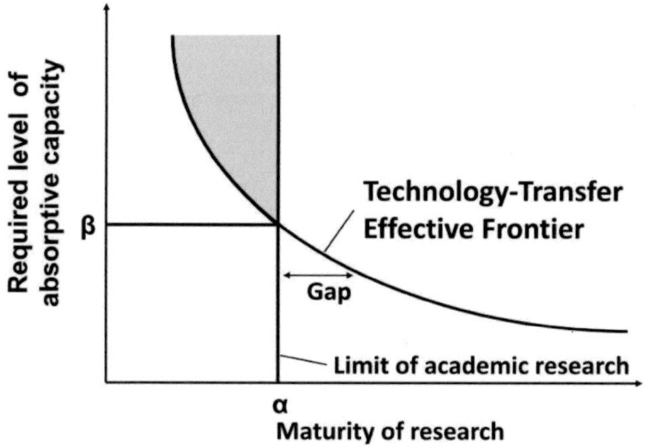

Figure 2: Concept of Gap in UIL

Figure 3 illustrates the three types of "bridging path" classifications shown across α on the x-axis. The issue for corporate strategy and management is how to develop collaboration so as to extend university research and commercialize it beyond the α level.

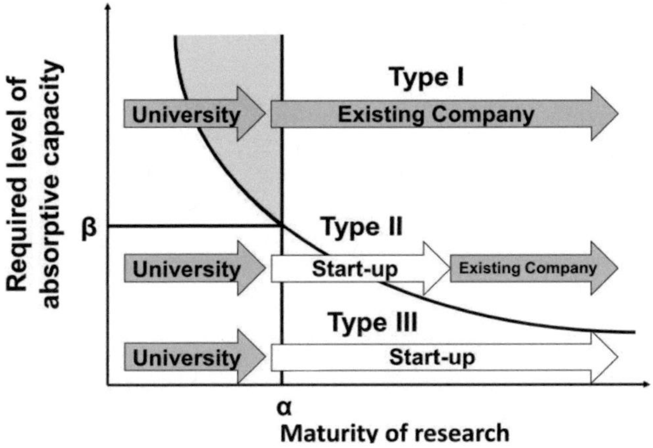

Figure 3: Bridging path classifications

- **Type I bridging** exists when the company can absorb science directly from the university through joint research. Most traditional Japanese UILs belong to this type of collaboration. The corporate strategic problem is how to enhance the firm's absorptive capacity.
- **Type II bridging** exists if a gap between the university and an industrial firm must be bridged by an intermediary such as a start-up company. A start-up unit has to extend the academic research to bring it within the firm's absorptive capacity. An in-house venture unit within a firm can perform this intermediary function if it is assured substantial autonomy.
- **Type III bridging** exists if extending the research will never lead to the business domain of an existing company. Therefore, new industries and firms must be created to absorb those areas to continue the research and realize its industrialization.

These three bridging paths are theoretically introduced from two premises, the technology-transfer effective frontier and the limited maturity of the university. Each bridging path depends on the nature of the technology and the ability of receiver-specific solutions to resolve issues between the technology provider and receiver.

The Generalized Concept of "Effective Frontier" for TA

The concept of this type of capability threshold and its solutions as the technology matures could be applied to other stakeholder relationships, especially in the early stages of research. To expand this concept from a *technology-transfer effective frontier* to a *technology assessment (TA) effective frontier*, we must address the following points.

Profiling a stakeholder's value chain and activities

It is necessary to identify a target stakeholder's main interests and describe the complete process to meet their interests that are independent of a scientific and technological evaluation. To break down the total process for TA and understand the activities in each process, a value chain analysis covering both upstream and downstream activities is essential. The value chain analysis provides information about a stakeholder's critical interests and provides goals and benchmarks.

Integrate a stakeholder's major interests and technology insight as their capability

Since the capability threshold concept is based on the integrated capabilities of both a firm's major interests and its technology evaluation, these two must be synthesized.

Introduce "the concept of threshold" to a stakeholder's "required capability"

The capability threshold concept is based on the threshold of the stakeholder's "required capabilities" to communicate with innovators and to understand the technology from their viewpoint at a given stage of technology maturity. The threshold itself continuously decreases as the technology matures, representing the TA effective frontier.

Determine the point at which the R&D maturity creates a critical issue for both an innovator and a stakeholder

At some stages of an innovator's activities, there are choke points or bottleneck points restricted by the characteristics of the stakeholder or innovator. For example, in the technology transfer model, the university is limited by how long it can continue research beyond a certain maturity. Innovators must also meet regulatory standards to start clinical development for medical products. These are the typical bottlenecks in R&D activity for innovators. In other word, stakeholders must address and/or control these choke points.

Describe the interactions between an innovator's and stakeholder's activities as an interaction path:

The *TA effective frontier* could divide the space into "*effective space*" and "*ineffective space*," which explains why a stakeholder's capability inevitably delays technology maturation. When a technological development progresses to a critical point of maturity without reaching the stakeholder's benchmark, the interaction path enters ineffective space and falls into the recognition gap.

Explain a specific event or phenomenon using an Interaction Path

Finally, this framework could be applied to explain real cases of innovator and stakeholder interactions in the case of a failure. However, this would require a careful description of the interaction path and whether the stakeholder's capabilities are positioned within the upper threshold at the critical point. Unless it exceeds the threshold, the innovator and the stakeholder could not communicate well in the effective space, and if the stakeholder has control over the research, its activity will fall into the recognition gap. A method drawn from organizational science may be appropriate to analyze the communication. The figure 4 integrates these elements to illustrate the framework.

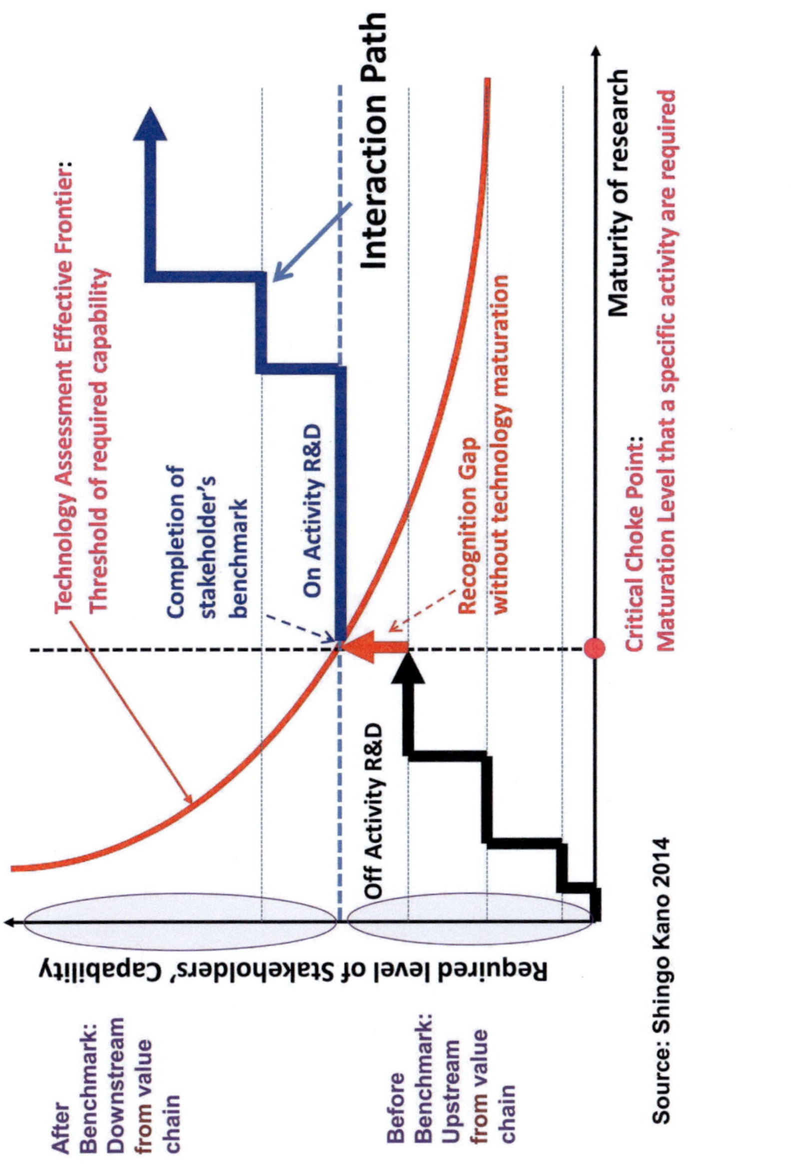

Figure 4: TA effective frontier framework

An Application to Innovator-Regulator Relationships

The TA effective frontier concept also applies to innovator–regulator relationships. The Research Institute of Science and Technology for Society (RISTEX) in Japan has implemented a project based on this concept, "Scenario Planning to Create Regulatory Policies and Technical Standards in Advanced Medicine" from 2013 to 2016.

There are many stakeholders in the medical field, such as research funding agencies, university researchers, medical product and/or service companies, patent agencies, regulatory agencies, investors, insurance organizations, physicians, hospitals, and patients, and the most powerful stakeholder, the regulatory agencies, who not only need scientific and technological insight but also can take a broad view to create regulations for medical products and services. Figure 5 illustrates the application of this concept to this case.

The project started by profiling the regulatory agency activities and a value chain analysis. The scope of the case study includes identifying the regulator's benchmarks, checking the innovators' bottleneck points, and organizational approaches using the boundary organization concept to clarify the interaction between innovators and regulators and the reason behind the gap. While this project has only just started, the outcome could provide a good example of the application of the TA effective frontier.

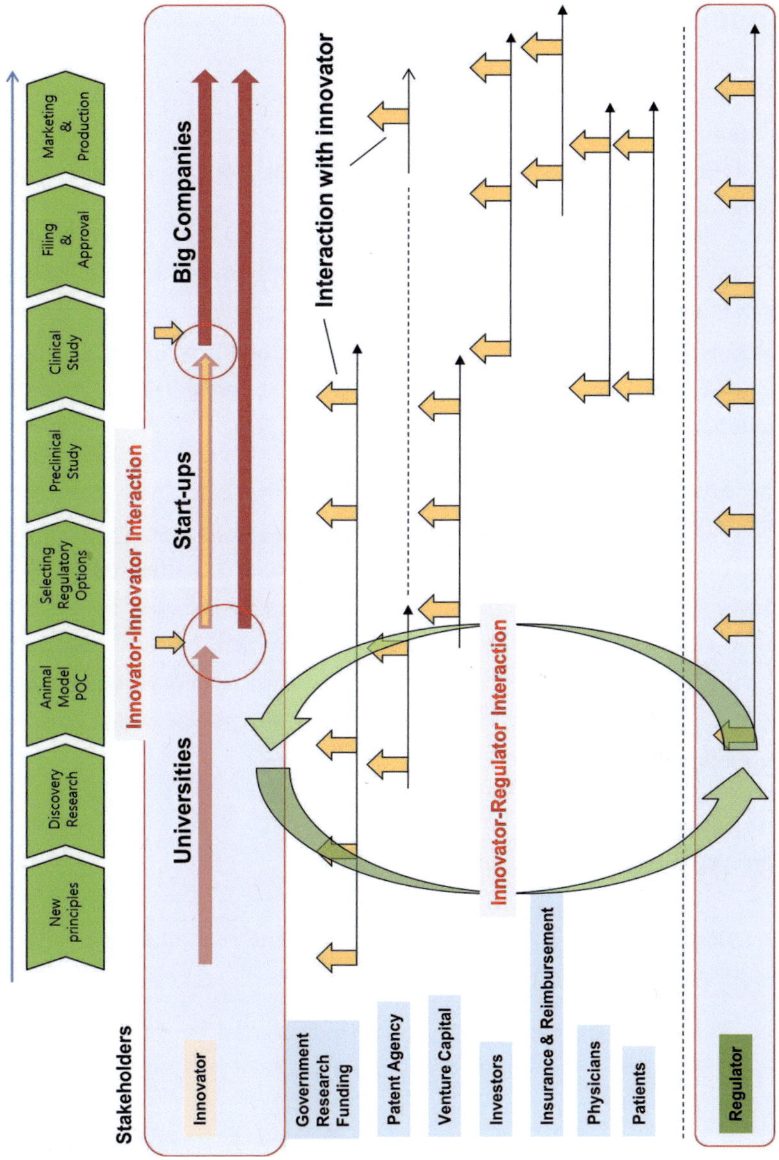

Figure 5: Stakeholders' activities with innovator

Conclusion

This chapter has introduced the *technology-transfer effective frontier* for technology provider–receiver interaction to explain the concept of capability thresholds and to demonstrate that this decreases as technology matures.

Secondly, this framework was extended to apply to an analysis of the interaction between TA stakeholders to a *TA effective frontier* framework accounting for other considerations, including profiling a stakeholder's activities, the threshold of required capabilities, research limitation points, and the interaction path concept.

The TA effective frontier is a general framework for explaining the limitations of stakeholders' capabilities at a given technology maturity that is capable of providing an analysis of various TA situations with a variety of types of stakeholders. The trajectories described as interaction paths visualize the recognition gap between stakeholders and also provide the clues to potential solutions. The applicability of this framework is now being validated against innovator–regulator interactions in the medical field.

References

Atkinson, S.H. (1994). "University-affiliated venture capital funds," Health Affairs, 13 (3):159–175

Coates, J. F. (1976). Technology assessment – A tool kit. Chemtech (June): 372–383

Cohen, W.N. and Levinthal, D.A. (1990). "Absorptive Capacity: A New Perspective on Learning and Innovation," Administrative Science Quarterly, 35(1): 128–152

Decker, M. and Ladikas, M. (Eds.). (2004). Volume 22: Bridges between science, society and policy technology assessment – methods and impacts. TAMI Project. Berlin: Springer Verlag. ISBN: 3-540-21283-3

Kano, S (2001). "Introduction and Comparison of Technology Transfer Models in University-Industry Relations: The Concept of Technology-Transfer Effectiveness Frontier and Its Application." Business Model (Electronic Journal of Japanese Society for Business Model) 1 (1): 1–10

Porter, A. L. (1995). "Technology assessment," Impact Assessment, 13: 135–151

Zahra, S. A., and George, G. (2002). "Absorptive Capacity: A Review, Reconceptualization, and Extension." Academy of Management Review 27 (2):185–203.

Technology Assessment Activity at the National Diet Library of Japan

Shinichi Kobayashi

Introduction

In Japan, the history of technology assessment (TA) activities for the national government and the Parliament is still short. However, since the necessity of such TA activities is being reviewed in foreign countries, the National Diet Library (NDL), which is an institution of the Japanese legislature, has begun to discuss the necessity of TA activity. Its TA activity was started in concrete form in 2010. This paper relates the background and the present state of adoption of TA activity at the National Diet Library.[65]

Among TA activities, those conducted for the government and the Parliament have a clear purpose. Their purpose is to explain the consequences that each featured technology will have on the government and its wider impact on our society. Inevitably, these TA activities must be objective in a sense different from that observed by the research activities conducted by ordinary researchers. In other words, TA needs to be a thorough and balanced analysis of critical technological innovations that affect our society, the environment, and the economy.

---

65 In Japan, the English expression of *Kokkai* (Parliament) is the "National Diet," which sounds slightly archaic. In this paper, the national library attached to the parliament is referred to as the National Diet Library, or NDL. However, *Kokkai* is referred to as the Parliament in this paper unless otherwise necessary for the convenience of readers.

Japan is one of the countries that lead the world in the field of science and technology, and the NDL, which is the principal library of Japan, naturally holds Japan's largest collection of scientific and technological information.[66] The collection includes an enormous volume of scientific and technological data such as the doctoral dissertations of Japanese universities and the reports of research results obtained under grants-in-aid from the Ministry of Education, Culture, Sports, Science and Technology, in addition to books and academic journals in the field of science and technology. However, it is little known that the NDL not only holds such scientific and technological information, but also has investigative and analytical functions concerning science and technology.

The NDL is required to respond to the diverse needs of society. In particular, its greatest mission is to provide services to the Parliament and related bodies. Among such services, TA activity is still very modest both in terms of time and experience, and even NDL does not refer to it as parliamentary TA. The recognition of this activity in Japan and abroad is therefore not high. Nevertheless, its intent and activities should not differ substantially from parliamentary TA in Europe and the United States.

This chapter is intended to describe the intent and activities of the NDL and to deepen the discussion on TA activity conducted for the national government, Parliament, and related bodies.

[66] The National Diet Library has both the function of the Parliament's library and that of a national central library. In addition, since Japan does not have a national science library, the National Diet Library holds books, magazines, and other material in all fields.

Discussion on the Necessity of TA Activity at the National Diet Library

In 2004, the National Diet Library formulated its "Basic Plan for the Development of Science and Technology Information – Execution of Immediate Tasks and a Library Structure after Reorganization."[67] In this plan, "Services for the Parliament and Related Bodies[68]" were positioned at the beginning of response to diverse needs. Those items contain the following statement: "In recent years, various issues on science and technology have become important issues of national policies, on which references requested by the Parliament have more focused. The services for the Parliament in such areas are characterized by the fact that policy-related information that meets national policy tasks and issues, rather than pure science and technology data, is required.

"To sufficiently fulfill our library's functions designed to contribute to legislation and deliberations on science and technology, we will further strengthen the following activities." And, "pursuing the enhancement of information on science and technology contained in publications of the Research and Legislative Reference Bureau" is listed as one of the specific activities to be strengthened.

To deliberate on the improvement of the scientific and technological information system at the NDL, the Council on Organization of Materials on Science and Technology (present Council on Organization of

---

67 The National Diet Library, "Basic Plan for the Development of Science and Technology Information – Execution of Immediate Tasks and a Library Structure after Reorganization (2004 – 2006)," 2004.1. (in Japanese). http://dl.ndl.go.jp/view/download/digidepo_1000920_po_maintenance_plan.pdf?contentNo=1

68 The phrase "Parliament and Related Bodies" refers to the House of Representatives, the House of Councilors, their members, committees, and Secretariats, political parties, and so on.

Science and Technology Information) was established at that time. In December, 2004, the council formulated its "Recommendation on the future of science and technology information system at the NDL in the electronic information environment"[69] in accordance with the Basic Plan for the Development of Science and Technology Information.

The recommendation also contained an item on strengthening the library's function of assisting in the legislative activities of the Parliament. In this item, it is recommended that: "the National Diet Library should seek to expand its function of providing assistance to legislation from the viewpoint of both enhancing information resources, including electronic information, and securing human resources. In terms of human resources, in particular, NDL should seek to develop and augment personnel having scientific literacy for appropriately providing scientific knowledge and specialized information to members of Parliament and those related to the Parliament on issues concerning science and technology." It goes without saying that this recommendation positions not only the provision of assistance to legislation at the Parliament, but also the dissemination of information such as "responding to the needs for information on various scientific and technological topics in which the population will be broadly interested, such as the environment, medical care/pharmacological affairs, nuclear power generation and natural disasters," and contribution to "developing children as bearers of the future of our society's science and technology," both of which have a complementary relationship with the provision of assistance, as important tasks.

69 Council on Organization of Materials on Science and Technology, "Recommendation on the future of science and technology information system at the NDL in the electronic information environment," 2004.12. (in Japanese) <http://dl.ndl.go.jp/view/download/digidepo_999250_po_teigen.pdf?contentNo=1>

In addition, this recommendation indicates recognition of the change in circumstances, stating: "Greater emphasis is being placed on the shift toward fusion or integration between science and technology and other fields, humanities and sociology, in particular, from the classical idea centering on science and technology. In fact, in many cases approaches that integrate a scientific and technological viewpoint and an economic and social viewpoint are required for solving national problems and citizen-level everyday problems." It further indicates: "NDL must fulfill its role of bonding science and technology with society by providing objective information for making decision on the positive and negative impacts of science and technology on people's life to the venue of national policy deliberations, and directly transmitting it to the population."

Such indications are based on almost the same recognition as the arguments in which a revival of the congressional TA function is expected around the same time in the United States.[70] In other words, the reality of science and technology and society in the twenty-first century has stirred up similar arguments, making it inevitable that such an argument would also be started in Japan. Additionally, a wave of these arguments has accelerated the start of TA activity at the National Diet Library in Japan.

Strengthening of TA Activity at the National Diet Library

Of course, this does not mean that no TA-like activity had been conducted at the NDL before then. For example, an irregular feature series

70 In the U.S. Congress, an argument calling for the revival of the Office of Technology Assessment (OTA), which was an organization attached to the Congress, continued after it was abolished in 1995. The Government Accountability Office (GAO), another organization attached to the Congress, has been the body officially responsible for TA since the fiscal year 2008.

entitled “Political Challenges over Science and Technology” has been published in “Research and Information – ISSUE BRIEF,” a periodical publication of the NDL.[71] In addition, the publication had once introduced TA activities conducted overseas.[72]

However, in response to the above arguments, the Research and Legislative Reference Bureau[73] of the NDL has considered it necessary to clarify the features of NDL’s services for the Parliament and the fields of research on which the NDL would place particular focus in the future. The NDL identified science and technology as one of these fields.

In this policy, it was decided to strengthen the NDS’s research on science and technology “select important national policy issues on science and technology, conduct research in cooperation with external intellectuals and specialized organizations, and prepare reports. NDL will also conduct the commissioning of part of the tasks to external bodies including the translation of reports prepared by TA institutes in other countries.

---

71 “Political Challenges over Science and Technology 2009,” Research and Information – ISSUE BRIEF, No.633, February 2009; “Political Challenges over Science and Technology 2007,” Research and Information – ISSUE BRIEF, No.563, February 2007; “Political Challenges over Science and Technology 2004”, Research and Information – ISSUE BRIEF, No.459, November 2004.

72 Meitetsu Haruyama, “Parliamentary Technology Assessment as a Dialogue between Science & Technology and Society,” Reference, No.675, April 2007, pp.83-97. (in Japanese) <http://www.ndl.go.jp/jp/diet/publication/refer/200704_675/067505.pdf>; Hisanori Tanaka, “Technology Assessment in the U.S. Congress,” Reference, No.675, April 2007, pp.99-115. (in Japanese) <http://www.ndl.go.jp/jp/diet/publication/refer/200704_675/067506.pdf>

73 In Japan, the research function for providing assistance to legislation has been placed in NDL, just like the United States ha the Congressional Research Service (CRS) in the Library of Congress (LC). This is the Research and Legislative Reference Bureau. The secretariats of the House of Councilors and the House of Representatives have divisions responsible for legislative research there as well as at the NDL. While the research function of the secretariats of the Houses is mainly research on legislation, the bureau is broadly in charge of all kinds of research on administrative oversight and assistance to legislation.

NDL will strengthen its research structure, for example, by setting up an office that assumes the central role." Implementation of this policy took the form of the launch of a Science and Technology Project and the establishment of the Science and a Technology Research Office[74] in FY2010.

In particular, with regard to the "translation of reports prepared by foreign TA institutes," NDL was expected to conduct its activity of providing assistance to legislation while translating reports prepared by U.K., German and other countries' parliamentary TA institutes and constantly watching overseas trends of TA. However, after several introductory papers[75] were published, the translation or introduction of foreign reports has not yet been implemented.[76]

As mentioned earlier, behind these considerations there is a lack of technology assessment in a broad sense that has a function of providing assistance on legislation or a function of research on science and technology, as indicated in the above-mentioned recommendation in 2004 by the Council on Organization of Materials on Science and Technology.

---

74 The Research and Legislative Reference Bureau consists of two lines of researchers: research service offices and research divisions. Research service offices conduct important research and assure the quality of divisions' researches. The divisions conduct regular research on request. Among the 15 divisions, the Education, Culture, Science and Technology Division covers fields of science and technology policy as well as education policy. The Science and Technology Research Office was established as a part of the Education, Culture, Science and Technology Division. One of the missions of the Science and Technology Research Office is to manage the science and technology projects, while several research service offices supervise the projects. Two or three researchers belong to the Science and Technology Research Office, while two or three visiting researchers assist in steering the science and technology projects.

75 Terumasa Oiso, "Parliamentary Technology Assessment in Different Countries: Focus on Germany," Reference, No.726, July 2011, pp.49-66. (in Japanese), < http://www.ndl.go.jp/jp/diet/publication/refer/pdf/072603.pdf>

76 This does not mean that the introduction of foreign TA reports has been excluded from its business. The NDL may introduce foreign TA reports, as necessary, in the future.

In other words, expectations are still present that TA activities in a broad sense from a contemporary perspective will continue in Japan.

Science and Technology Project

Major research activities conducted by the Research and Legislative Reference Bureau of the NDL are divided into three types: research in response to requests by the Houses and their Members, anticipatory research, and project-type comprehensive research.[77] In research in response to requests from legislative bodies, committees, and members of Parliament, research on politics, the economy, national policy challenges from the public at large, circumstances and systems in Japan and abroad, and other topics is conducted in a short time period. These activities are intended to reply to individual request, and none of the contents of the activities are published. The NDL replies to approximately 40,000 various major and minor requests every year, and some of these requests are related to science and technology. In contrast, anticipatory research activities are conducted voluntarily based on forecasts of possible national policy issues. The results are published in three publications: "Research and Information – ISSUE BRIEF", "Reference" and "Foreign Legislation"[78].

---

77 Under the National Diet Library Act, research conducted on request and anticipatory research are prescribed. Project-type comprehensive research is a form of anticipatory research. However, since it is conducted by a team of interdisciplinary researchers, and to distinguish it from ordinary research conducted by one or a few researchers, this paper classifies and introduces comprehensive research as the third category.

78 These publications are available not only to those related to the Parliament, including members of parliament, but also to the general public through the Internet. In addition to these publications, NDL holds "Policy Seminars" for members of parliament, their staffs, and other Parliament staff members to provide them with information. However, this information is not available to the public.

Project-type comprehensive research is also a form of anticipatory research in terms of its content and formal category. For each of cross-sectoral topics, a cross-bureau project team is formed to conduct research for approximately one year, and a report on the results is issued as a publication entitled "Research Material." In these activities, topics from science and technology are covered in some cases. Recently covered topics included "Regeneration of Japan through technology and culture" (2012), "Policy response to the Great East Japan Earthquake and problems" (2012) and "Building a sustainable society" (2010). These publications have been posted on the web page of the NDL.

Apart from the above-mentioned research activities, a project-type research activity called "Science and Technology Project" is under way. This has been conducted every year since FY2010.[79] In this project, NDL selects important topics from a variety of topics related to science and technology, looking forward several years into the future, and organizes a research committee consisting of external experts according to the topic, and the committee works on research and analysis in cooperation with an independent policy institute.

Parallel to this, NDL researchers in sectors related to the topic gather within NDL in a cross-bureau manner to prepare a report based on field research, interviews, literature review and other undertakings. For those sectors and viewpoints requiring manpower in addition to the office researchers, experts from universities and the like are invited to serve as visiting researchers or part-time researchers and to conduct research. The topics so far are as shown in Table 1.

[79] The author took part in the activities of the Science and Technology Project for three years (FY2010-FY2012) as a visiting researcher. Since FY2013, he has worked for the NDL as a full-time senior specialist, supervising the Science and Technology Project.

Table 1: List of topics of the Science and Technology Project, FY2010–2014

FY2010	Science and Technology Policy System; international perspective
FY2011	Public Research and Funding System
FY2012	Ocean Science and Technology
FY2013	Renewable Energy System
FY2014	Cyber Security

*These reports are all written in Japanese only and are available on the website of the NDL.
FY2010: http://www.ndl.go.jp/jp/diet/publication/document/2011/201003.pdf;
http://www.ndl.go.jp/jp/diet/publication/document/2011/201004.pdf,
FY2011: http://www.ndl.go.jp/jp/diet/publication/document/2012/index.html,
FY2012: http://www.ndl.go.jp/jp/diet/publication/document/2013/index.html,
FY2013: http://www.ndl.go.jp/jp/diet/publication/document/2014/index.html

The NDL is not a research institute like universities or national laboratories. The task of its staff is to provide "information on science and technology" that can be used as reference for Parliament's deliberations. The staff conducts research on technological issues, the present state of systems and regulations related to such issues, and trends in research activities and their future directions, and extracts the impact on future policies and the expected roles of the legislative bodies.

Further, they organize the prospective impact on the economy and everyday life, future possibilities, the necessity of institutional and political responses, and so on. In doing so, they also scrutinize similar arguments in foreign countries. Thus, the team of the "Science and Technology Project" prepares unique reports that cover various issues from the basics of science and technology to politics and sociology. These reports differ not only from research papers or descriptions in the field of science and technology, but also from descriptions of laws and regulations or systems.

Significance of NDL's TA-like Activity

The National Diet Library conducts TA-like research activities because much of Parliament's deliberation on budgets and accounts and its legislative activity is naturally related to science and technology policies and the government's research activities. This has long remained unchanged. However, the amount of legislation submitted by Parliament members[80] has recently increased. Table 2 shows examples of recent legislation related to science and technology at the instance of Parliament members.

80 In legislative activities in Japan, bills are classified into three types according to the submitter: Cabinet bills (bills submitted by the Cabinet), Upper House bills (bills submitted by Upper Parliament members), and Lower House bills (bills submitted by Lower Parliament members). Among them, Lower House bills and Upper House bills are collectively called legislation by Parliament members. In Japan, Cabinet bills have traditionally represented the largest proportion. However, recent legislation by Parliament members has also been actively conducted.

Table 2: Examples of legislation related to science and technology at the instance of Parliament members

Year of promulgation	Act
1995	Science and Technology Basic Act
1997	Act on Organ Transplantation
1999	Basic Act on the Promotion of Core Manufacturing Technology
2002	Basic Act on Energy Policy
2006	Cancer Control Act
2007	Basic Act on Ocean Policy
	Basic Act on the Advancement of Utilizing Geospatial Information
2008	Aerospace Basic Act
	Basic Act on Biodiversity
	Research and Development Enhancement Act *
2009	Basic Act for the Promotion of Biomass Utilization
2013	Act on the Promotion of Regenerative Medicine **

* The full title of the act is "Act of Strengthening R&D Capability and Efficient Promotion of R&D with Promotion of R&D System Reform."

** The full title of the act is "Act on the Promotion of Comprehensive Measures to Realize the Quick and Safe Provision of Regenerative Medicine Treatments."

Concerning newly emerging problems and cutting-edge science and technology, there are cases where it is uncertain which administrative body is responsible or multiple administrative bodies are involved, delaying the start of legislation. If the legislative bodies are responsible, it is possible to promptly and flexibly pursue legislative activity from a broad viewpoint. Thus, the enactment of acts related to science and technology through legislation by members of Parliament is rational. However, it is necessary for the members to fully understand, discuss, and assess issues related to science and technology. Nevertheless, many members are unfamiliar with science and technology, and they do not easily keep up with recent trends even if they have expertise in some areas.

If a member of Parliament does not have much information on matters under discussion that are related to science and technology, such as that needed for making a decision, the service of the NDL that provides legislative information would be an effective tool. Researchers at the NDL commit themselves to organizing the necessary information and providing it in a well-balanced manner, including specialized information such as research papers written by domestic and foreign scholars.

The second significant fact is that science and technology has spread into every corner of modern society and our lives and that consequently there are a growing number of issues related to science and technology in parliamentary research and deliberation on national policies. In addition, public R&D funding has long been on the increase, and scientific and technological activities are supported by society and the government.

Science and technology have now become inseparable from the nation and society, and vice versa. As a result, many policy issues have a connection in some form with science and technology. For example, the fact that the Fukushima Nuclear Accident Independent Investigation Commission (NAIIC) was established in the Parliament in order to conduct an investigation and make a recommendation for determining the cause of the accident at the Fukushima Daiichi Nuclear Power Plant of Tokyo Electric Power Company on March 11, 2011, is still fresh in our memory. The NAIIC is said to be the "first independent investigative body for Japanese people that was established in the Parliament in the history of the Japanese constitutional government." The Committee's report, published in July, 2012, recommended that "A system for appointing independent investigation committees, including experts largely from the private sector, must be developed to deal with unresolved issues."[81] Although this recommendation has not been realized

81 The National Diet of Japan, "Executive summary, Recommendation 7: Develop a system of independent investigation commissions," The official report of The Fukushima Nuclear Accident Independent Investigation Commission, July 2012, p.23.

yet, it can be said that a system for assisting research and deliberation on national policy issues at the legislative body is now also required in various fields in Japan.

The third item of significance is inextricably linked to the second point described above. It has become necessary for those involved in politics to have an interest in science and technology precisely because science and technology have now spread into society as well as the fact that the Parliament needs to make full and appropriate use of information regarding science and technology for national policy deliberations.

It can be said that the development of today's science and technology is supported not only by scholars but also by society, the economy, the population, and the Parliament. In addition, the whole of society has the responsibility to pass science and technology as a cultural asset on to the next generation, and the Parliament also bears part of this responsibility. Therefore, it is necessary to transmit not only the information provided by scientists and engineers, but also the opinions and attitudes of the business community, society, and the population on scientific and technological activities to the Parliament and its members in a smooth and well-balanced manner.

Although TA activity at the NDL has just started, it can be said that the perspective described above is exactly the same as the significance of the presence of parliamentary TA in other countries.

<http://warp.da.ndl.go.jp/collections/NDL_WA_po_print/info:ndljp/pid/3856371/naiic.go.jp/wp-content/uploads/2012/09/NDL_WA_po_NAIIC_report_hi_res10.pdf>

Enhancing Relationship with other TA-like Activities in Japan

NDL's TA-like activities do not have a formal relationship with other TA-like activities in Japan due to the accounting system and other restrictions. However, the NDL is studying how it can have a collaborative relationship with potential partners, and it is possible that there may be some form of collaboration with them in the future.

To build collaboration with other TA-like activities in Japan, it is necessary to overcome major challenges. The most important one is that those in academic circles understand the characteristics of assistance provided for legislation and its difference from assistance given to administrative bodies.

In Japanese society, it is not uncommon for those in academic circles, including university scholars, to submit reports including recommendations from their professional viewpoints. However, it should be noted that most of these proposals are submitted to administrative bodies. In many cases, such proposals also contain recommendations concerning matters directly related to policies, such as what kinds of policies should be implemented and how policies should be changed. In quite a lot of cases, they also contain evidence that supports a certain policy.

Reports submitted to the legislative bodies are prepared for members of Parliament, who represent the people, and are also open to the people, who had elected the Parliament. The legislative body is the place where the members of Parliament elected by the people conduct legislation. Reports submitted to the members of Parliament and the Houses must not be intended to urge a specific legislative act, but should definitely provide materials or evidence offering assistance for preparing legislation. Instead of proposing policies themselves, these reports should mainly be analyses of the present issues, possible issues, and/or alternatives.

Especially importantly is that proposals presented to the administrative body are allowed to contain particular content, but that reports intended to provide assistance for legislation are balanced information that contains a possible alternative policy or inconvenient evidence, not a particular policy or merely evidence that supports it. One of the important roles of the legislative bodies is administrative oversight. In that sense, the NDL is required to provide not only evidence supporting a certain policy but also inconvenient evidence in a well-balanced manner before the members of Parliament make their judgment. Therefore, the evidence provided to the legislative bodies in legislative information and based on expertise, has more significance than recommendations or reports presented to an administrative body.

It used to be the case in Japanese society that an administrative body made all the decisions and pursued them. In such a society, academic circles found their significance in presenting proposals or conveying requests to the administrative body.

However, in pursuing TA-like activities as a legislative assistant, not only the NDL but also its outside partners must radically change the framework of its approach from that taken in providing assistance to an administrative body. This will also provide an opportunity for academic circles and TA-like activities in Japan to change dramatically. Realizing close collaboration between the NDL's TA-like activities and other TA-like activities in Japan would also be of significance for other TA-like activities in Japan as a whole.

Conclusion

Compared internationally, it can be said that the National Diet Library already has a function as a parliamentary TA organization in a substantive sense. Its future task will be to heighten its recognition and presence by steadily increasing its experience and achievement and by earning the trust of all stakeholders for its function of providing assistance for legislation concerning science and technology in general.

Authors

Nuno Boavida graduated in Industrial Production Engineering at the Universidade Nova de Lisboa in 1999, and did a M.Sc. in Industrial Relations and Personnel Management at the London School of Economics and Political Science in 2001. After his graduation, he has been involved in the publication of books and other scientific publications, as well as in reports and evaluations to the European Commission. Presently, Nuno Boavida finished his PhD thesis in Technology Assessment on "Decisions of Technology innovation: the use of indicators" at the Universidade Nova de Lisboa. He is a researcher at the Interdisciplinary Centre of Social Sciences of the Universidade Nova de Lisboa (CICS.Nova), and an invited researcher of the Institute of Technology Assessment and Systems Analysis of the Karlsruhe Institute of Technology.

Christian Büscher, Sociologist. Started his academic career at the University Bielefeld, Faculty of Sociology where he got his Diploma in Sociology and post-graduate at the college "Technology and Society" TU Darmstadt, Germany (PhD Dissertation 2003). Since 2006 he is Senior Scientist at the Institute for Technology Assessment and Systems Analysis (ITAS), Karlsruhe Institute of Technology (KIT). Former positions were: consultant (Technologieberater) at VDI Technologiezentrum GmbH (German Engineers Association), Department of Research, Technology and Innovation, Düsseldorf, Germany; Senior Researcher at alpS - Centre for Natural Hazard and Risk Management,

Innsbruck, Austria. His current research interests are systemic risk, sociotechnical systems, and energy system transformation.

Armin Grunwald is Professor Dr. rer. nat. and studied physics, maths, and philosophy at the universities of Münster and Cologne. In 1987 he finished his dissertation on thermal transport processes in semiconductors at Cologne University. From 1987-1991 he acted as systems specialist in software engineering. In 1991-1995 he was researcher at the DLR (German Aerospace Center) in the field of technology assessment. From 1996 - 1999 he was vice director of the European Academy Bad Neuenahr-Ahrweiler. Since October 1999 Armin Grunwald is director of the institute for Technology Assessment and systems analysis (ITAS) at Karlsruhe Institute of Technology (KIT). Since 2002 he is also director of the Office of Technology Assessment at the German Bundestag (TAB). Since 2007 he also holds the university chair of philosophy of technology at KIT. His working areas are: theory and methodology of technology assessment, ethics of technology, concepts and theory of sustainable development.

Shinichiro Izumi is Director General, Research Institute of Science and Technology for Society (RISTEX)

Shingo Kano is Associate Professor of Bio-Innovation Policy Research Unit, Department of Computational Biology and Medical Sciences, Graduate School of Frontier Sciences, The University of Tokyo, Japan. His current interests are University-Industry relations as a head of Biotechnology Intellectual Property Educational Course and the member of Intellectual Property Committee at University of Tokyo; the interaction between innovators and regulators in the medical field such as regenerative medicine and personalized medicine; and public policies in advanced medical field including international comparisons. Currently he is serving on the editorial board of the journal Japanese MOT society.

Atsuo Kishimoto is currently a project professor of Graduate School of Public Policy (GrasPP) and Policy Alternative Research Institute (PARI), The University of Tokyo. His research covers a broad scope of safety and regulation, including risk assessment, risk governance, economic analysis, Regulatory Impact Assessment, etc.

Shinichi Kobayashi is a senior specialist at Bureau of Research and Legislative Reference of National Diet (Parliament) Library, Japan. He earned BA in 1979, MA in Policy Sciences in 1982, and PhD candidate in Policy Sciences in 1986 at University of Tsukuba. He has worked for various universities and research institutes including a Research Director of National Institute of Science and Technology Policy (NISTEP), a Director of RISTEX Research Center at Research Institute of Science and Technology for Society (RISTEX), a Director of Center for Technology and Society at National Institute of Advanced Industrial Science and Technology (AIST). He has worked in the field of social and policy studies in Higher Education and Science and Technology.

Makiko Matsuo is currently a project researcher of Graduate School of Public Policy (GrasPP) and Policy Alternative Research Institute (PARI), The University of Tokyo. Her areas of concern are interdisciplinary in nature and cover such issues as, Risk Governance, Risk

Regulation, and Food Safety, Interface Issues between Science and Politics, Technology Assessment (TA), International Standards Setting Process, International Harmonization etc.

Masahiro Matsuura is a researcher at the Graduate School of Public Policy, The University of Tokyo.

Christina Merz holds a University degree in Sociology, Criminal Law and Educational Science at the University of Tübingen (Germany). She works as a researcher for the Institute for Technology Assessment and Systems Analysis (ITAS) at the Karlsruhe Institute of Technology (KIT). Her current research agenda focuses on the assessment of Big Data technologies and the role of technology in law enforcement.

António B. Moniz is a sociologist graduated at the University Institute of Lisbon (ISCTE-IUL) in 1980. Was lecturer at the University of Azores (Portugal) from 1980 until 1983, and since then is teaching at University Nova Lisbon, UNL (Portugal) where he is professor (PhD diploma from 1992 and habilitation from 2001) at the Faculty of Sciences and Technology. From 2011 he is also senior scientist at ITAS, Karlsruhe Institute of Technology (Germany). Was member of the Program Committee of the Targeted Socio-Economic Research (TSER) of the European Commission (4FP). He is co-ordinator of the Doctorate Programme on Technology Assessment at the Faculty of Sciences and Technology (UNL) since 2009. He is the founder of the national Observatory of Technology Assessment (OAT) in Portugal in 2015, of the national network on TA (GrEAT) in 2010.

Akira Morita is the Program Director of the Science for Science, Technology and Innovation Policy project and Director-General of the National Institute of Population and Social Security Research (Japan).

Kumi Okuwada is a Senior Fellow, National Institute of Science and Technology Policy (NISTEP), and Affiliated Fellow, Research Institute of Science and Technology for Society (RISTEX). She is also Visiting Professor, Graduate School of Knowledge Science, Japan Advanced Institute of Science and Technology (JAIST). She engages in management of a funding program on "Science for Science, Technology and Innovation Policy". She was a former Director of Science and Technology Foresight Center of NISTEP in 2007-2011. She conducted the 9th science and technology foresight project in Japan during 2008-2009 FYs, in response to the request from the Council of Science and Technology Policy. She was also a chief editor of monthly reports of "Science & Technology Trends" which has introduced advanced technologies to policy-makers and communities in science and technology. She has also guided PhD candidates of knowledge science course in JAIST and other universities, using her long experience as a researcher in a private company. She has published many papers on foresight studies and in ICT field. She has also some patents on nanoelectronics, materials and processing.

Constanze Scherz studied social sciences at the Humboldt University Berlin. Since 2008 she is scientist at the Institute of Technology Assessment and Systems Analysis (ITAS) in the Karlsruhe Institute of Technology (KIT) and the editor of the journal "Technology Assessment – Theory and Practice". From 2002-2008 she worked at the Office of

Technology Assessment at the German Bundestag. Her main research topics are knowledge society, knowledge in processes of policy advice, and parliaments and civil society in TA.

Masashi Tachikawa is a professor at the College of Agriculture, Ibaraki University in Japan. His major field of interest is risk governance issues of emerging technologies, such as biotechnology and nanotechnology.

Taketoshi Taniguchi is a Professor at UTokyo Policy Alternatives Research Institute (PARI), the University of Tokyo. Prior to joining UOT in 2012, he was the Director of the Socio-Economic Research Center at the Central Research Institute of the Electric Power Industry from 2005-2010. He received his Ph.D. in nuclear engineering from the University of Tokyo in 1984. He is a founder and served as a representative of HSE Risk C-cube, an NPO for risk communication and collaboration with the communit1y from 2005 to 2012. Since 2015, he serves as a research advisor of Research Institute of Science for Safety and Sustainability of National Institute of Advanced Industrial Science and Technology, and as a member of Director Board of the Hitachi Global Foundation. Dr. Taniguchi's area of expertise includes energy and nuclear policies, energy-related environmental risk and external cost analysis, organizational risk management and the societal decision-making process. Recent main research concerns are risk governance of technological systems in highly interconnected and interdependent world, all hazards national risk assessment and strategic foresight for building future resilient Japan.

Masaru Yarime is Project Associate Professor of Science, Technology, and Innovation Governance (STIG) at the Graduate School of Public Policy of the University of Tokyo, Japan. He also has an appointment as Honorary Reader in the Department of Science, Technology, Engineering and Public Policy (STEaPP) of University College London, United Kingdom. His research interests focus on public policy, corporate strategy, and institutional design for promoting science, technology, and innovation for sustainability. He received B.Eng. in Chemical Engineering from the University of Tokyo, M.S. in Chemical Engineering from the California Institute of Technology, and Ph.D. in Economics and Policy Studies of Technological Change from Maastricht University in the Netherlands. Previously he worked as Senior Research Fellow at the National Institute of Science and Technology Policy (NISTEP) of the Japanese Ministry of Education, Culture, Sports, Science and Technology (MEXT).

Go Yoshizawa Ph. D. is Associate Professor of Biomedical Ethics and Public Policy at the Graduate School of Medicine, Osaka University. He holds MSc and PhD in Science and Technology Policy from University of Sussex, UK and MSc in History of Science from University of Tokyo. Having experience of working at a private think-tank and several universities, he has been involved in a number of projects on technology assessment, science communication and public engagement, knowledge policy and management in life and medical sciences as well as in the fields of environmental and energy.